THE VIETNAM WAR IN RETROSPECT

THE
VIETNAM WAR
IN RETROSPECT

Four Lectures

by

Martin F. Herz

School of Foreign Service
Georgetown University
Washington, D.C.

Library of Congress Cataloging in Publication Data

Herz, Martin Florian, 1917-
    The Vietnam War in Retrospect

    1. Vietnamese Conflict, 1961–1975—Addresses, essays,
lectures. I. Title.

DS557.7.H47   1984   959.704'3   83-20600
ISBN 0-934742-28-6

Printed in the United States of America

School of Foreign Service
Georgetown University
Washington, D.C. 20057

Contents

Foreword

Peter F. Krogh

Dean, School of Foreign Service, Georgetown University

Because of a grave illness, Ambassador Martin Herz had been unable to meet his scheduled class on the Cold War during the spring semester 1982; and in the fall, when he had greatly improved, he not only resumed his regular teaching but came to me offering what he called "perhaps my final contribution to the School of Foreign Service" in the form of a special series of lectures on the Vietnam War in retrospect. Held in November and December in the late afternoon in our new auditorium, they represented a kind of "co-curricular" remedial teaching. In other times they might have been termed a "teach-in." The lectures were well attended—but how different was the atmosphere from the days when the Vietnam conflict was such a subject of hot contention on the campuses!

Many were surprised when the lectures began with pictures of the Vietnamese countryside and of people at work and at play, and when the lecturer offered historical anecdotes and invited his listeners to "make a leap of the imagination" and put themselves in the place of Vietnamese in certain situations. Ambassador Herz also used cartoons and some of the prize-winning photos of the war to illustrate his points. These are not, in other words, dry academic lectures but highly personal experiences. Ambassador Herz had a point of view on how things fitted together and why certain decisions were taken; and he didn't mind reaching back, in order to make a point, to personal experiences in places far removed from Vietnam.

These lectures thus represent a kind of "testament" left to us by an American diplomat-historian who did not consider himself an expert on the Vietnam War even though he had dealings concerning it over a long period of time, in Paris, Phnom Penh and Washington and, during an important eighteen-month assignment, in Saigon. I myself would consider him an expert. He had for many years maintained files on the conflict, had written on the subject, and had almost every important book on the war in his personal library. In any case, he was an acknowledged expert on something more important. Twenty years ago, Ambassador Herz, then on a sabbatical at the Foreign Service Institute, gathered together the essential items of information about the origins of the Cold War and produced a book (*Beginnings of the Cold War*) that was acclaimed for its evenhandedness and objectivity because he tried to show how certain things looked from the Russian as well as the American perspective.

In the present instance he also tried to show how certain things looked from the perspective of the other side, but his approach is not evenhanded. It is that of an outspoken critic—his criticism being directed less at those who got the United States into the war (he demonstrates, to me quite plausibly, that it would have been almost inconceivable for us not to have helped South Vietnam) than it is directed at sloppy thinking, willful denial of obvious facts, lack of historical knowledge and perspective, and interesting instances of dishonesty that in his view attended much of the past discussion of the conflict and also the reporting about it.

It is a useful learning experience, and a highly stimulating one. Martin Herz did not shun controversy. Nobody was bored listening to him. If the reader is left with a better understanding of how things hang together in recent history then this publication will have achieved its purpose. The Vietnam War has had a tremendous impact on our psyche and thus on our nation's ability to act on the world scene. I therefore believe that anything that allows us to understand the conflict better represents also a contribution toward the goal of every good diplomat and every good educator in foreign affairs, which is to help in making the world a less dangerous place.

* * * * * * * * * *

Postscript. On October 5, 1983, while this manuscript was in the process of publication, its author, Martin F. Herz, died of cancer at the Georgetown University Hospital. A brief résumé of his career appears at the end of this, his last, publication. Some additional observations are, I feel, in order here.

Martin Herz was noted for his personal courage and outspokenness, his extraordinary sense of public service, and his brilliance as an editor and analyst. He possessed a mind and a determination to use it that overwhelmed subject matter ranging from the history of Cambodia, to the history of the Cold War, to the verities of international politics, the determinants of regional politics and the requirements of the conduct of diplomacy.

He used his exceptional natural abilities to the fullest. He continually educated himself. He placed himself at the service of his government. He fought for freedom. He devoted himself to the cause of making the world a less dangerous place. He left behind, for oncoming generations, a rich legacy of writings. He established an institution, the Institute for the Study of Diplomacy. He permanently embedded himself in the hearts of his closest friends. That is a formidable, enviable record.

Lecture One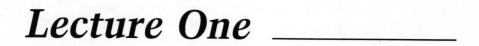

I WILL TRY TO TELL YOU about the war in Vietnam as I have come to understand it on the basis of my experience in the U.S. Foreign Service. I served in Paris (1950–54) during the First Indochina War, the war in which the French tried to hold onto their colonial possessions. Then I served in Cambodia (1955–57) after the Geneva Agreement that ended the First Indochina War, and I learned there about the profound political realignment that was going on in neighboring South Vietnam. Later I was in charge of Lao and Cambodian affairs in the State Department (1967–68) and then served as political counselor in Ho Chi Minh City, then called Saigon (1968–70), from just after the "Tet" offensive in 1968 to just before the invasion of Cambodia in 1970. But I think the most important contribution I can make to an understanding of our involvement in Vietnam comes from my first-hand experience and study of the origins of the Cold War, for it is quite certain that if there hadn't been a Cold War we would never have become involved in Vietnam.

Disaster for All Concerned?

I think it is fair to say that the Indochina Wars were a disaster for all concerned, but it isn't enough to make a flat statement because there are important distinctions. Certainly the Vietnamese suffered tremendously. Out of a total population of a little over 40 million, north and south, close to a million must have died in the Second Indochina War alone, the part in which we became directly involved. And of course this doesn't count the wounded and crippled or the millions who were displaced, and the hundreds of thousands in Vietnam who are still suffering because of the war. In America, although we lost only 58,000 killed, which is about the number of people in our country who die every year in automobile accidents, the war caused grievous harm and human anguish, and the wounds it left in our society are not yet healed.

But when one says the war was a disaster for all concerned one really has to recognize that it was not a disaster at all for the Soviet Union. Without losing a single soldier the USSR managed to humiliate the United States, and by keeping the war going contributed to the near-disintegration of our polity—our political society—in the late 1960s and early 1970s, which was to them a benefit in itself, quite aside from the acquisition by the Soviet navy of one of the finest naval bases in the world, the one that we built at Cam Ranh Bay, which now projects Soviet military power into the Indian Ocean and the South Pacific.

Also, without in any way wishing to be critical of them, I think it can be said that for Japan the American involvement in Vietnam was an economic bonanza.

In addition to our heavy military expenditures in their country, the Japanese also benefited from our program of inflation control in South Vietnam. Our presence there involved the spending of so much local currency that there would have been a runaway inflation in South Vietnam if we had not helped to import consumer goods so that money in circulation could find things to buy. So there was a quite unheard-of situation in South Vietnam where during a war the availability of consumer goods increased manifold. The Japanese motorbike and tricycle, the Japanese outboard motor and sewing machine, transistor radio and TV—all these became ubiquitous in South Vietnam, especially in the Mekong Delta during the war.

So one can't really say that the war was bad for everybody. The immediate participants paid in lives and suffering and terrible dislocation, but some nations benefited very much. It is even said that by holding the Communists at bay in South Vietnam, the United States gained for other Southeast Asian countries like Indonesia the time they needed to consolidate their independence. I don't know if this is really so. But it is certainly true that the repercussions of the war in Vietnam were tremendous not only in Vietnam itself and in the United States but also in other places very far removed from Southeast Asia. For instance American policy toward Africa in the 1970s can only be understood in terms of what our experience in Vietnam did to us as a nation. In many indirect ways we still have to contend with the legacy of Vietnam.

Some people have talked about a "Ten Thousand Day War" as if the American war in Indochina had been just a continuation of the French war, which in my opinion it was not at all. Yet the two wars were closely interrelated, because in a sense one gave rise to the other. I will try to explain to you how the events in Indochina were connected with Vietnam's history, with our history, and with things that happened very far away.

For everything in history hangs together, especially in these days of rapid communications when there are superpowers with worldwide interests and hair-trigger weapons. As I shall explain, I think the war in Korea in the early 1950s had a great deal to do with how we looked at Vietnam and why we got in. Our interests in Europe also had a great deal to do with it. And of course the most important factor was our relationship with the Soviet Union. When we fought in Vietnam we didn't just fight the Vietnamese Communists, we were also up against the tremendous logistic system of the USSR which for long periods of time was shoveling in materiel faster than we could destroy it from the air or on the battlefields.

So the task I have set myself in these lectures is to illuminate the Vietnam War from a wider perspective, and also from the perspective of someone who was there and helped to close out the American commitment. Don't misunderstand me: By "closing out" I mean that I am proud of my part of the effort to end the war and to end our involvement in it in an honorable fashion. We failed in that endeavor, but failure was not inevitable.

All right, let us now look at the contestants, the adversaries, and see where they came from, with what perceptions they encountered each other. Do not fear that I will treat you to a long historical disquisition; this is just going to be a kind of character sketch of the principal protagonists on the basis of the national experiences that shaped their views of the world, of themselves, and of each other.

Some Things That Make Vietnamese Tick

The Vietnamese, or their predecessors, were an unruly tribe in the southern reaches of China who were subjugated and incorporated into the Chinese empire in 111 B.C. Over a thousand years later, in 938 A.D., the Vietnamese rose and drove out the Chinese, under the command of Ngo Quyen, a venerated hero about whom every Vietnamese learns in school. Historians are not at all clear how it came about that after a thousand years of Chinese rule, from which they benefited so much, and during which they had become practically indistinguishable from the Chinese, the Vietnamese should have asserted a national identity that had not really existed before the arrival of the Chinese.

At any rate the Chinese did not accept this declaration of independence for very long, and when the Sung dynasty came into power they prepared to reconquer Vietnam. For a while a *modus vivendi* was worked out whereby 1) the Vietnamese accepted Chinese overlordship [suzerainty] in return for Chinese assurances of internal autonomy and self-administration, without any Chinese military presence; 2) the Chinese allowed Vietnamese dynasties to rule in their own territory in return for acknowledgment of their status as vassals; and 3) the Vietnamese had to send a triennial mission carrying tribute to the Son of Heaven, adopt the Chinese calendar and laws, and follow Chinese foreign policy (which did not mean very much since China did not have important interests in the area around Vietnam).

Now, let us stop for a moment and look at the implications of that situation: The Vietnamese got the substance of what they wanted, namely independence in all internal respects, with their own government and without the presence of foreign troops; but they yielded to the Chinese in symbolic matters like tribute, acknowledgment of suzerainty, calendar, etc. It should be noted that at the time that we are talking about, Vietnam was not yet called Vietnam and was confined to the area of the Red River delta, roughly the northern part of what for a while was known as North Vietnam.

The Chinese invaded Vietnam in 980 and were defeated, and the threepoint formula of suzerainty was re-instituted. The Chinese invaded again in 1079 and were again defeated, and again the compromise arrangement was re-instituted. In 1257 the Mongols demanded passage through Vietnam in order to attack the armies of the Sung dynasty from the south. They were defeated and driven back into China. Yet another time, in 1284, the Mongols demanded transit through Vietnam, this time to attack the kindgom of Champa to the south. They were again defeated, this time by Vietnamese forces led by Tran Hung Dao.

5

I think you are beginning to get the idea why I am citing this distant history: because this is what goes into the making of Vietnamese national consciousness. Perhaps it is becoming apparent why the Vietnamese see themselves as good

Tran Hung Dao

fighters who have braved the onslaughts of far superior armies and prevailed against them. Every Vietnamese school child knows the story of Tran Hung Dao who was among those convoked by the king of Vietnam when the Mongols demanded submission. If we fight we shall all be killed, the king said; but if we submit we shall be slaves. What should we do?

And Tran Hung Dao, the doughty soldier, raised his spear or shield or sword or whatever they raised in those days, and he shouted: "Your majesty, if you wish to surrender then cut off my head first, for while it remains on my shoulders the kingdom shall stand." And all the assembled nobles and warriors, with one voice, shouted "We Will Fight!" I don't know if you choke up when you hear this story—probably not, because you are not Vietnamese; but perhaps you can imagine how inspiring the story must be to a young Vietnamese. There was a bit of Tran Hung Dao in some of the Vietnamese who fought the French, and later in the South Vietnamese guerrillas and North Vietnamese main force soldiers who fought against the Americans.

The March to the South

I projected on the screen this section of an old map of Southeast Asia not because it is accurate—it is in fact wildly inaccurate although very decorative— but because it shows that in the sixteenth century, when this map was made in Europe, the principal country on the Indochina peninsula was considered to be Champa, which occupied the central part of what today is Vietnam. (The little Vietnam of the early sixteenth century occupied part of the area labeled "Cachuchina" on this map.) Champa (spelled "Çampa" on the old map) is one of those many countries in world history that were defeated and subjugated and whose populations were dispersed in such a manner that one can say, with very little exaggeration, that they disappeared from the face of the earth. Champa was a mighty empire of Hindu civilization with magnificent temples and palaces, all of which were completely destroyed by the Vietnamese, so that only a few of the foundations remain.

Champa was in the way of Vietnam's expansion to the south, and after centuries of seesawing battles and invasions and counterinvasions starting in the eleventh century, the "final solution to the Champa problem" came only in 1693, when the last remnant of that once mighty empire was annihilated. So another element in the Vietnamese national consciousness is the unrelenting push

6

to the south, what the Vietnamese call *Nam Tien,* and which has a counterpart in what the Germans used to call *Der Drang nach Osten,* the urge to expand to the east. The Vietnamese have had this urge to expand to the south, which carried right into the twentieth century. Saigon was a Cambodian village less than two hundred years ago. In fact, after today's central Vietnam was taken away from Champa, all of what today is the southern part of Vietnam was taken away from the Cambodians. *Nam Tien* had something about it comparable to our slogan of "manifest destiny" in the nineteenth century. If it hadn't been for the arrival of the French in the middle of the last century, all of Cambodia would have been divided between Vietnam and Thailand.

16th Century Map

A word about Vietnamese national unity or, rather, the lack of it during the country's turbulent history. In the early seventeenth century Vietnam divided into a northern portion ruled by the Trinh dynasty and a southern portion ruled by the Nguyen. The British historian P.J. Honey relates what then happened in the following terms: "By 1620 the break . . . had become an established fact and two massive defensive walls were constructed by the southerners at Dong Hoi and Truong-Duc, not many miles from the line (DMZ) established by the 1954 Geneva accords." For the next fifty-three years there were attacks by the North trying to subjugate the South. "The last attack was repulsed in 1674, after which the two rival states lived through roughly a century of what today, in modern parlance, would be termed 'Cold War,' enjoying neither trade nor diplomatic relations with each other."

Toward the end of the eighteenth century the country was reunited by the so-called Tay Son rebellion. The last heir to the Nguyen dynasty made a deal with the French, and they helped him gain control first of Cochinchina, as the *southernmost* part of Vietnam was then called, then Annam in the center and finally, but only temporarily, Tonkin in the north. This happened in 1802 and it was the first time the country had been unified all the way from Tonkin to Cochinchina in the south. But the southern emperor, Nguyen Anh, never fully pacified the North, which was effectively occupied only later, by the French.

Now, why am I telling you all this? Is it really necessary for an understanding of the war? I would submit that it is very relevant because even this thumbnail history teaches us a number of things. It is clear that the Vietnamese have a warlike nature and tradition. What we have learned about *Nam Tien,* the march

7

INDOCHINA
circa
1885-1954

David Hagen

to the south, explains quite a lot about the historical foundations on which the Communist regime in Hanoi could build. We have also learned about the difference between Tonkin in the north, and Annam in the center, and Cochinchina in the south, each with a separate history and each, incidentally, treated very differently by the French. We have seen that there has been a prolonged and very deep split between the North and South, between the followers of the Trinh and the followers of the Nguyen; and the split, which runs throughout their history, is of course a reflection of the important personality differences between northerners and southerners. We Americans should have some sympathetic understanding of such differences since we have had them in our own country, and one could draw parallels with the histories of many other countries. Only, in Vietnam the North fought the South for fifty years and then was totally cut off from it for another hundred years. Such things leave scars, and of course they also explain why people develop in different directions.

I found an interesting reference to this difference between northerners and southerners in the book *Fire in the Lake* by Frances FitzGerald, which was an influential book in the internal battles in the United States about our involvement in Vietnam. It is evident from the introduction to the passage that I shall quote that Ms. FitzGerald did not particularly like references to such differences, which she called "clichés" But as she herself shows, the matter was far more than that; it involved and still involves today pretty fundamental attitudes and character traits. Here is what Ms. FitzGerald wrote:

> The Vietnamese need no anthropologist to tell them that there are differences between northerners and southerners. The differences are clichés, endless source of jokes and, occasionally, of hostility. One southern member of the Viet Minh who had regrouped to the north in 1954 under the terms of the Geneva Agreements gave examples of these clichés in describing the relations between the northerners and the southerners in his unit. The southerners, he said, "are used to being free and extravagant in their expenses. After working hours they get together and go eat or play guitars and sing." The northerners on the other hand, "are very economical in their expenses and not very generous in their relations with friends." While the southerners

8

like to fight among themselves and to argue about matters of policy, the northerners "obey their leaders, and in the meetings they are ready to respond to any motto or any way. . . . [They] try to keep their present positions and thirst for fame." The difference in life-style, said the soldier, provoked continual arguments within the unit. "Those northern stinkers are miserly," the southerners complained. "They consider money as a big wheel. They are cowards like land crabs. . . . [They are] servile flatterers, always nodding to show their submission and never conceiving any idea of fighting for their rights." The northerners in anger blamed the southerners for never being satisfied with anything and for fighting among themselves all the time. "Those southern guys," they said, "only know how to have fun. They do not have Revolutionary Ethics. Their fighting standpoint is weak."

Change a word here and there, and you have pretty much the difference between the Germans and the Austrians: The northerners are disciplined, somewhat lacking in imagination, inflexible, courageous, the "Prussians" with their own rigid system of values; whereas the southerners are faction-ridden, individualistic, hard to discipline, life-loving, slower, a bit more imaginative and self-centered.

Every country is a prisoner of its history, of how it has collectively experienced the world. Vietnamese history has made the people—northerners and southerners—by and large distrustful of foreigners and distrustful of their own governments, a bit devious, and inclined to prefer complicated explanations to simple ones. But their history has also made them freedom-loving and very confident in their strength and their capacity to prevail. And their experience with the French, which ended with the French army suffering a devastating defeat in 1954, contributed to the feeling that the Vietnamese, who had beaten the Chinese and the Mongols and the French and who had destroyed Champa and torn off chunks of Cambodia, were quite able to deal with the Americans who, in the Communist view, were just successors to the French colonialists.

Impact of World War II

I don't think there would be much point in discussing the French administration of Vietnam, for in terms of the Vietnamese perceptions it must be clear to everyone that especially after World War II the French hold on the country was perceived as an anachronism and an affront to Vietnamese national honor. But there were some special factors. First among those factors was the humiliation of the French at the hands of the Japanese who occupied Vietnam in 1940 and left the French in charge to administer the country for them. Later, after France was liberated from the Axis in 1944, the French in Indochina tried to rise against the Japanese, but the Japanese got wind of their plans and simply clapped the French into prison camps. One doesn't have to be an Oriental to imagine what this must have meant in terms of loss of face.

At the end of the war, the country was occupied by the Chinese in the north

9

and by the British in the south. But the Vietnamese declared their independence in September 1945, and the Viet Minh, the Communist-dominated freedom fighters against the French and the Japanese, began eradicating what they called

Lee Lockwood/Black Star

Ho Chi Minh

"reactionary elements" throughout the country. I want to draw attention to this because we encounter here for the first time the concurrence in time of two related but distinct activities: The fight for liberation on one hand, and efforts to do in one's internal political opponents on the other. War against foreigners and civil war can go hand in hand, as we had found for instance in Greece and Yugoslavia and China during World War II. The list of Vietnamese democratic, non-Communist freedom fighters assassinated by the Communists is a long one.

The British upon their arrival in Cochinchina, the southern part of Vietnam, released the French from their imprisonment and turned over the administration of the colony to them. This turned out to be a great mistake, for even the relatively mild South Vietnamese had absolutely no desire to see the French colonial regime revived. The French landed troops and under General Leclerc, a hero of World War II in Africa, began what they called the "pacification" of Vietnam. The British withdrew in 1946. There was still a Democratic Republic of Vietnam in Hanoi, in the north, under a certain Ho Chi Minh, but that government was operating on sufferance of the Chinese occupation—and in those days the Chinese were not Communists but still the so-called Nationalists under Chiang Kai-shek.

To everyone's surprise, Ho Chi Minh invited the French back into North Vietnam, as a means of getting the Chinese out. There was considerable opposition to that move, and it is recorded what Ho Chi Minh said to his colleagues to justify what he had done:

> You fools! Don't you realize what it means if the Chinese stay? Don't you remember your history? The last time the Chinese came, they stayed one thousand years! The French are foreigners. They are weak. Colonialism is dying out. Nothing will be able to withstand world pressure for independence. They may stay for a while, but they will have to go because the white man is finished in Asia. But if the Chinese stay now, they will never leave. As for me, I prefer to smell French shit for five years, rather than Chinese shit for the rest of my life.

You may wonder if I'm ever going to get to the war that the United States fought in Vietnam, but I hope you understand that I am trying to give you a bit of the flavor of national perceptions, of the complex situation in which the United States became involved. It is all very well to say that Ho Chi Minh was a Communist and that the Viet Minh were dominated by the Communists, but I think it is apparent that when the Democratic Republic of Vietnam next negotiated with the French about the status of Vietnam within the so-called French Union, it did so in a spirit of patriotism and proud asssertiveness. The negotiations collapsed, the French attacked the Viet Minh, there was bad faith and treachery on both sides—but the thing that is frequently left out of the equation by people who chronicle war is that, once more, it was a triangular affair.

Ho Chi Minh and his Communists, although they formed temporary alliances with other nationalist organizations in the fight against the French, actually fought a civil war even while they were fighting for national liberation. It is one of the many tragedies of that first Indochina war that the Communists systematically betrayed rival nationalist fighters who were not Communists to the French, and that there were even some democratically inclined Vietnamese who temporarily fought on the French side against the Vietnamese Communists because they thought that there was a better chance for freedom after a French victory than after a Communist victory.

The Korean War and Vietnam

As far as the United States is concerned, a landmark in our perception of Vietnam was the outbreak of the Korean War in 1950. The Communists had taken over China the year before and were by now funneling arms directly to the Viet Minh. When the North Koreans attacked South Korea it was clear in Washington that this could not have happened without encouragement and support from Moscow and Peking. It was seen as part of a coming broad Communist offensive. At the time we still saw Russia and China as closely united, as indeed they were during that initial period.

Washington addressed the invasion of South Korea in terms of its worldwide policy of containing Communism. So when President Truman made his first decision to support South Korea, he ordered five steps: The U.S. Air Force was to give all-out support to the South Koreans south of the 38th parallel; U.S. forces in the Philippines were to be strengthened; the Seventh Fleet was to be interposed between Taiwan and the mainland; a new resolution was to be introduced in the United Nations asking members to give South Korea help in repelling the attack and to restore peace; and *aid to the French in Indochina was to be increased.*

When one hears about this today it seems a bit strange to us: Why help the French in Vietnam, Laos and Cambodia in 1950 because the North Koreans attacked the South Koreans over two thousand miles away? That requires some explaining. I think the matter is highly relevant to what we are discussing here because the war in Korea had important repercussions *in Europe* that influenced American attitudes toward what the French were trying to do in Indochina; for from the perspective of Washington containment required a concerted effort to stem the advance of Communism everywhere on the perimeter of the Communist world. I will come back to the connection between American policy toward Indochina and Europe in a little while.

11

Everybody, or almost everybody, knows that the French were finally beaten in Indochina, but many people do not know that the Viet Minh victories were largely in the north. Dien Bien Phu, site of the climactic battle in 1954, is deep in the mountains of North Vietnam. It is doubtful that the Viet Minh would have been able to defeat the French in the Mekong Delta area in the south where the Communist stock was not so high, partly because the Viet Minh had antagonized the religious sects, the Hao Hoa and the Cao Dai, and the armed forces of the Binh Xuyen who fought on the side of the French puppet emperor, Bao Dai.

Dien Bien Phu was a tremendous feat of arms, for it was a site which the French themselves had chosen for a showdown in the belief that they could decimate any attacking force with their superior artillery and could stand their ground indefinitely because they could supply themselves from the air. To the surprise of the French and everyone else, the Vietnamese with Chinese assistance manhandled heavy artillery over the mountains and into concealed position all around; they obtained clear superiority from the beginning, including interdiction of the air space over Dien Pien Phu; and they methodically ground down the French defenders with vastly superior firepower, finally taking position after fortified position in infantry charges prepared by sappers who burrowed trenches right up to the French lines.

The siege of Dien Bien Phu was already under way when the Geneva Conference took place in April 1954. There was a government crisis in Paris, and Pierre Mendès-France promised to settle the entire Indochina question within thirty days if he became Prime Minister, else he would resign. Thus the French in effect operated under a self-imposed deadline. At one time the clocks in the conference hall in Geneva had to be stopped, so the agreement could still be concluded before expiration of the deadline. There was a widespread belief that the Geneva Agreements that ended the First Indochina War were suprisingly favorable to the French, considering that they had suffered such a humiliating military defeat during the conference. One month later, Prime Minister Mendès-France helped defeat the project of a European army in the French National Assembly.

The Geneva Agreement of 1954

It is important to note the basic elements of the Geneva Agreement of 1954 because there have been charges that the United States was associated with their alleged violation by South Vietnam. The Geneva Agreement called for a division between North Vietnam and South Vietnam along the seventeenth parallel, with establishment of a so-called Demilitarized Zone between them. This was to be a temporary demarcation line pending the holding of elections two years later, in 1956. In the meantime the agreement provided that the French would pull out of North Vietnam and the Viet Minh would pull out of South Vietnam. There was to be a free movement of populations allowing them to choose in which of the two parts of the country they wished to live. And the agreement provided for an international control commission (composed of India, Poland and Canada) which was to supervise the implementation.

The Geneva Conference was attended by the USSR, China, Great Britain, France, the United States, North Vietnam and South Vietnam, but the agreement was concluded only between France and North Vietnam. The United States only declared that it would not disturb the agreement, otherwise it wanted nothing to do with it. But the most important aspect that is often overlooked is that South Vietnam refused to sign as well. At that time South Vietnam barely existed as an entity. It was generally regarded as a creation of the French that would disappear in short order; but it showed a surprising independence from the French by actually denouncing the agreement and especially the part calling for elections in 1956, because there were no provisions for international supervision to insure that those elections would be free. Shortly after Geneva the South Vietnamese government showed even more independence by forcing the abdication of the French puppet emperor Bao Dai, establishing a republic, and asking the French to get out.

So ended the First Indochina War. (I am passing over the parallel developments in Laos and Cambodia, which had complexities of their own, because we are concentrating here on Vietnam.) What did that war and its outcome mean to the world and to the relationship between the great powers? Professor Hans J. Morgenthau has in my opinion summarized the matter admirably when he wrote about the ''paradoxes'' of the Geneva Agreement. He wrote this in 1956, before he became a passionate opponent of American policy in Vietnam. I consider this summary of the worldwide implications of the First Indochina War to be quite dispassionate. Here is what he said:

> Take the . . . paradox concerning the objectives for which the war was fought. For France, this was essentially a colonial war, no different than the wars that France and Spain were engaged in in Africa in the 1920s. For the great majority of Vietnamese, it was a war for national liberation. However, for those who made that war possible in the first place, that is to say, the Soviet Union and Communist China, the war had nothing to do with national liberation or colonialism. It was an attempt to extend the sphere of influence and domination of communism.

> Conversely, for the United States the war was neither a colonial war nor a war of national liberation. Certainly the United States did not support France for the purpose of maintaining French power in Indochina. For the United States, too, the main issue of the war was the expansion of communism. In other words, for the United States the war was fought for the purpose of containing communism, as part and parcel of the overall world strategy which the United States had pursued from the beginning of the Cold War.

While agreeing with every word that Professor Morgenthau wrote on that occasion, I would like to add two observations: First, it is clear that the United States was not out of sympathy with the national aspirations of the Indochinese peoples—we in fact encouraged the French to grant them the widest possible degree of autonomy and even independence. Why then did we not push the French harder? We did not explicitly dissociate ourselves from the concept of a French Union, in other words from their aim to combine the granting of power to the Vietnamese with some remaining hold on the territory. This had to do with the fact that France was an ally of ours, and a very prickly one at that. And second, we needed French cooperation for the defense of Europe, which was in a precarious state in the early fifties. And Europe was and is a lot more important to the United States than Southeast Asia. I think it is not going too far to say—although it sounds paradoxical—that one reason we became involved in supporting the French in Indochina was our concern with the defense of Europe.

The French Perspective after Korea

It is hard to credit this in retrospect, but when South Korea was invaded in 1950 this created a wave of fear *in Europe* and a belief that in some way the aggression in the Far East foreshadowed also an onslaught of the Communist war machine in Europe. People were in a panic, and they looked to the United States for leadership not only in countering the aggression in the Far East but also in assuring the defense of Western Europe. All of a sudden the fact had to be faced that there were virtually no combat-ready troops facing the Russians. There were leaks in the newspapers that the NATO plan for the event of a Russian invasion was to retreat all across Germany and across France and to hold onto a perimeter in the Brittany peninsula, then called the "Breton Redoubt," somewhat analogous to the Pusan perimeter in South Korea to which we clung at first very precariously but which then enabled the breakout and the victory after MacArthur landed at Inchon and rolled up the North Korean forces.

To the Europeans such a strategy was anything but reassuring. Only five years after World War II they saw themselves confronted with the prospect of armies again rolling over their territories not once but twice—once during the retreat before the Russian hordes, then later when those hordes would presumably be pushed back, perhaps years afterwards. The American government acknowledged the misgivings of the Europeans but told them that a "forward defense" in Germany was simply not possible unless the Germans themselves were associated with the Western defense. At the time this was an almost heretical idea, for German militarism was still remembered as the enemy that had inflicted so much suffering on Europe. But the pressure for a German defense contribution grew not only in America but also in Europe.

Partly to get out of the dilemma, and partly from a genuine devotion to the idea of European federation, the French government then proposed an integrated European Army which would include Germany in the defense of Western Europe without actually authorizing the creation of a German army. I was one of the officers in the American Embassy in Paris who observed the slow progress, against tremendous obstacles, that the European Army project made first in negotiations for a European Defense Community treaty and then toward the hoped-for ratification of that treaty by the French parliament.

I am telling you about this because here you have before you someone who tried to look at the Indochina war also through French eyes. I personally had very little sympathy for what the French were doing in Vietnam, but I had to recognize that the cooperation of France was infinitely more important to the United States than any points that we might win with the Vietnamese nationalists. The French government desperately needed some support for the European Army from elements on the right of the political spectrum. But those were the very elements who trumpeted nationalist slogans about France's role as a great power and how it was being undermined by the Americans.

We supported the French during the First Indochina War partly because they were allies in Europe and partly to help counter the fears of nationalist Frenchmen that they would be overbalanced by the Germans in a European Defense Community.

The fact that we picked up a large part of the French financial burden in Indochina enabled the French government to say, "It isn't true that we are being bled white in Indochina, the war isn't costing us so much, we will be quite able to hold our own in any partnership which includes the Germans." There were very few of us in the American Embassy—I don't say that there weren't perhaps one or two, but there were *very* few—who didn't think the French were played out in Vietnam. Yet we were unhappy to see them beaten, because we feared a nationalistic reaction in Europe. So we were glad that the French obtained a pretty good deal in Geneva and that the U.S. contributed to it by our stiff anti-Communist position, also because we hoped that perhaps a possibility would now exist to save at least half of Vietnam from the Communists.

As I said, all this is not at all in contradiction to the analysis of Professor Morgenthau. It just supplements what he has written and gives perhaps a somewhat more rounded picture. Of course, as I have already mentioned, the European Defense Community was defeated in the French parliament shortly after Geneva. Paradoxically, that was followed a little while later by the admission of Germany to NATO as a full-fledged member with its own national military forces.

Aftermath of Geneva

The newly created South Vietnam, which was struggling to survive after the 1954 Geneva Conference, was a most unpromising proposition. The victor over the French was of course not South Vietnam but North Vietnam, the so-called Democratic Republic of Vietnam, and it was there, in the north, that there existed a new self-confidence and dynamism as the victors started to institute Communism and to eliminate their remaining internal enemies. Over one million people fled from the north to the south, mainly Catholics. Many non-Catholics also wanted to leave but lacked the organizational arrangements, and in the end the North Vietnamese authorities stopped the movement of people.

In the south a virtually unknown politician, a mystic nationalist mandarin named Ngo Dinh Diem, became prime minister and then president. He lacked the most elementary control over the country. There were religious sects who were waiting to take over territory abandoned by the Viet Minh. The Binh Xuyen, which was like a Mafia with its own uniformed army, had wound up in control of the Saigon police. The flood of refugees from the north placed an enormous burden on the government at the very time when the French administrators were leaving. It was no secret that only a part of the Viet Minh were withdrawn to the north; another part went underground and established arms caches throughout the country—no less than 3,000 such caches were found by the South Vietnamese authorities between 1954 and 1959, when the Second Indochina War began.

Very few people expected that Ngo Dinh Diem would be able to pull his country together, that he would be able to *make* a country of South Vietnam; and of course some expected that two years later there would be elections anyway and that since the more populous North Vietnam would vote 100 percent in favor of unification, a Communist takeover of the south was a foregone conclusion. President Eisenhower himself recalled later that in the immediate aftermath of the Geneva Agreement he estimated that if there were free elections in Vietnam, Ho Chi Minh would receive something like 80 percent of the vote. But the elections had been specified by the French and the North Vietnamese to be held only in 1956, and many things were to happen in the intervening time.

As a matter of fact, as we shall see, South Vietnam, contrary to all expectations, turned out to be a viable entity. Diem got rid of the French; he held a plebiscite and got rid of Bao Dai; he promulgated a new constitution; he asserted control over the sects and broke the back of the Binh Xuyen gangster fraternity. He gave the South Vietnamese some confidence in an independent future. He of course bitterly opposed nationwide elections in 1956. In the United States Senate, a young senator named John F. Kennedy pointed out that to hold elections throughout Vietnam when there was no reason to believe that any kind of freedom would exist in North Vietnam would be a farce and a betrayal amounting to a surrender of a country to Communism. The million refugees who had come from the north brought with them reports of the severities and even atrocities committed by the Communists in the course of the so-called land reform in which middle class elements were mercilessly uprooted, disinherited, and sometimes killed. Even the North Vietnamese government itself acknowledged that it had been guilty of "excesses."

In this situation, while it might have been true that Ho Chi Minh would have obtained 80 percent of the vote in 1954, when he represented the force that had obtained liberation from the French and when no other visible Vietnamese leadership existed, by 1956 the situation was very different. There was little doubt that however well the Communists might do in the north, they could not possibly obtain a majority in the south—not because people loved Diem but because they thought life under the Communists would be much more unpleasant.

This is a phenomenon that we will encounter again in the brief history of South Vietnam. It does not follow from the fact that a government might be unpopular that the people who want to overthrow it are popular. The Communists had given so much evidence of ruthlessness and cruelty, of duplicity and betrayal of allies and coalition partners, they seemed to be making such a hash of things in their own northern part of Vietnam, that there was little stomach in South Vietnam for reunification under Communism in 1956. And since South Vietnam had never signed the 1954 Agreement and had in fact protested against it at Geneva, Ngo Dinh Diem saw no reason to implement an agreement which was not binding upon him.

It must be difficult for you to put yourselves in the frame of mind of American policymakers in 1956 when South Vietnam was precariously maintaining itself and when the Communists were still digesting North Vietnam; but perhaps a glimpse of the thinking of some liberal Americans can be gotten from a speech that Senator John F. Kennedy made in September 1956. He said:

> Vietnam [of course, he meant *South* Vietnam] represents a test of American responsibility and determination in Asia. If we are not the parents of little Vietnam, then surely we are the godparents. We presided at its birth, we gave assistance to its life, we have helped to shape its future. As French influence in the political, economic and military spheres has declined in Vietnam, American influence has steadily grown. This is our offspring— we cannot abandon it, we cannot ignore its needs. And if it falls victim to any of the perils that threaten its existence—communism, political anarchy, poverty and the rest—then the United States, with some justification, will be held responsible; and our prestige in Asia will sink to a new low.

Less than five years later, the man who spoke those words became President of the United States.

Lecture Two ───────────

FOR THOSE WHO WERE UNABLE to attend the first lecture—and for any who may have fallen asleep—I would like briefly to recapitulate what we have learned so far. We have heard about the extraordinary soldierly qualities of the Vietnamese and their history of resistance to big powers and their tradition of *Nam Tien*, the push to the south. We have noted the difference of character and history between the northern and the southern parts of Vietnam. I have tried to explain why the Korean War had a very important influence on how the United States came to see developments in Southeast Asia, and how especially the repercussions in Europe from the Korean War had important consequences for American policy in Southeast Asia. We heard about the war of the Viet Minh against the French and how it ended with a French defeat and the Geneva Agreement, which gave the Communists only North Vietnam and left South Vietnam seemingly up for grabs.

I think I also explained how South Vietnam, the lonely waif at the Geneva Conference, turned out to have much more personality than anyone had expected; that Ngo Dinh Diem threw the French out and leaned on American support to build up South Vietnam against any threat from the North; and how a kind of feeling of paternity, or perhaps godfatherliness, characterized the early American attitude toward South Vietnam. That took us up to 1956, the year when according to the agreement between the French and the North Vietnamese elections were to be held throughout Vietnam which presumably would bring unification.

There were no such elections. And the fact that there were no elections had a very bad effect on the remaining Viet Minh in South Vietnam. Up to 1956 some people cooperated with them because they were afraid that come 1956 the Viet Minh and their masters in North Vietnam would run the country. But when people saw that South Vietnam was solidifying as an independent state, even increasingly receiving international recognition, many decided that it was now safe to turn in the Viet Minh who had gone underground; so the fortunes of the Communists in South Vietnam declined further—at least for a while.

How Diem Looked in 1956

Some of you may not know what the Pentagon Papers are. The U.S. Department of Defense undertook a big secret project of putting together a history of the Vietnam War that was to include the secret intelligence appreciations and policy decisions, in order to see what lessons might be learned from the past. These papers, part of which had been contracted out to a "think tank" in California, the Rand Corporation, were leaked to the press by Daniel Ellsberg, a Rand

21

employee who had turned from a strong proponent of the war into a strong opponent. Publication of the Pentagon Papers in 1971 was exceedingly embarrassing to the American government, particularly since the *New York Times* and the *Washington Post*, both of them strongly opposed to the war, naturally selected for publication the portions most damaging to the government.

I mention the Pentagon Papers because they contain what I believe is a very reasonable and rational appraisal of the situation in South Vietnam about a year or so after the Geneva Agreement. The passage that I will now quote also explains how the United States became more and more committed to the support of Ngo Dinh Diem despite his dictatorial qualities and his rather mediocre performance in fighting the Communists:

Ngo Dinh Diem

Whatever people thought of him, Ngo Dinh Diem really did accomplish miracles, just as his American boosters said he did. He took power in 1954 amid political chaos, and within ten months surmounted attempted coups d'etat from within his army and rebellions by disparate irregulars. He consolidated his regime while providing creditably for an influx of nearly one million destitute refugees from North Vietnam; and he did all of this despite active French opposition and vacillating American support. Under his leadership South Vietnam became well established as a sovereign state, by 1955 recognized *de jure* by 36 other nations. Moreover, by mid-1955 Diem secured the strong backing of the U.S. He conducted a plebiscite in late 1955, in which an overwhelming vote was recorded for him in preference to Bao Dai; during 1956, he installed a government— representative in form, at least—drafted a constitution, and extended GVN [Government of Vietnam, South] control to regions that had been under sect or Viet Minh rule for a decade; and he pledged to initiate extensive reforms in landholding, public health, and education. With American help, he established a truly national, modern army, and formed rural security forces to police the countryside. In accomplishing all the foregoing, he confounded those Vietnamese of North and South, and those French, who had looked for his imminent downfall.

While it is true that his reforms entailed oppressive measures —e.g., his 'political reeducation centers' were in fact little more than concentration camps for potential foes of his government—his regime compared favorably with other Asian governments of the same period in its respect for the person and property of citizens. There is much that can be offered in mitigation of Diem's authoritarianism. He began as the most singularly disadvantaged head of state of his era. His political legacy was endemic violence and virulent anti-colonialism. He took office at a time when the government of Vietnam controlled only a few blocks of downtown Saigon; the rest of the capital was the feudal fief of the Bihn Xuyen gangster fraternity. Beyond the environs of Saigon, South Vietnam lay divided among the Viet Minh enclaves and the theocratic dominions of the Cao Dai and the Hoa Hao sects. All these powers would have opposed any Saigon government, whatever its composition; in fact, their existence accounts for much of the confidence the DRV [Democratic Republic of Vietnam, North] then exhibited toward the outcome of the Geneva Settlement. For Diem to have erected any central government in South Vietnam without reckoning resolutely with their several armed forces and clandestine organizations would have been impossible; they were the very stuff of South Vietnam's politics.

Diem's initial political tests reinforced his propensity to inflexibility. The lessons of his first 10 months of rule must have underscored to Diem the value of swift, tough action against dissent and of demanding absolute personal loyalty of top officials. Also, by May 1955, Ngo Dinh Diem had demonstrated to his satisfaction that the U.S. was sufficiently committed to South Vietnam that he could afford on occasion to resist American pressure, and even to ignore American advice. Diem knew, as surely as did the United States, that he himself represented the only alternative to a communist South Vietnam.

What Triple-Canopy Jungle Means

I have not yet talked about what the country looks like, and I must do this now very briefly for the Vietnamese landscape is an important part of the story of the war. Vietnam is something very special, and it is difficult for someone who has never been there to imagine the terrain over which the war was fought. The country is, first of all, really quite rich. There is no great pressure on the land, certainly not in South Vietnam; farmers have two, sometimes even three harvests per year. The people are hardworking and this, combined with the extraordinary fertility of the alluvial soil in the Red River Delta in the north and the Mekong Delta in the south, plus the usual regularity of the rainy season, and large irrigation works where water may be lacking—all this makes for a rich agricultural country. Canals, especially in the southern part of the country, are an important feature of the terrain.

Although the Mekong Delta does not have much jungle it does have some patches of it and those areas are almost impenetrable. There is plenty of triple-canopy jungle in the

INDOCHINA
1954-1975

David Hagen

23

north of what was South Vietnam, and in the mountains of the center, and also in the south, especially along the Cambodian border and in the bottom tip of Vietnam. So there is jungle along all the border areas where the Communists sent from the north ''infiltrated'' the country. What such triple-canopy jungle means is perhaps best illustrated by a story.

Long before I came to Vietnam, when I was serving in Iran, I asked an American general who was running our military aid mission there why it didn't seem possible simply to erect a physical barrier that would prevent infiltration from North Vietnam into South Vietnam. Martin, he said, let me tell you how I experienced triple-canopy jungle during World War II when I was commanding an infantry unit in New Guinea. One day one of our artillery spotter planes went down in the jungle. We could see where it had gone down—in a valley where we had troops in the north and also at the southern end. So two battalions of infantry were sent out to find the plane, one going south in an extended line making their way through the jungle, and the other battalion coming up from the south to the north. At the end of the day, said the general, no member of either battalion had seen the plane—but what was more disquieting, no member of either battalion had met a member of the other battalion! That gives you an idea of the denseness of triple-canopy rain forests.

I myself have seen such forest in Cambodia, but I have only flown over it in Vietnam. From the air it looks like endless dense green heads of cauliflower crowding each other and leaving no space between them. I guess it can be seen that if you are going to play cops and robbers in the jungle, it is much easier to be on the side of the robbers than to be on the side of the cops who are supposed to find them.

An American Perspective on Vietnam and Communist Expansion

Now, having given you last time a sketch of some of the elements that went into the making of Vietnamese attitudes during the war, I think I still owe you also an outline of the principal factors that went into the thinking of American policymakers—and fortunately it is not necessary in this case to go back to 111 B.C. America's attitude toward Communism and toward the power of the USSR and China goes back only to World War II when we were allies of the Russians and the Chinese and looked forward to a long period of cooperative relations to preserve the peace of the world. We were disappointed in this when, even while the war was still going on in Europe, the Russians seemed to ignore agreements concluded at Yalta with regard to Poland—at least President Roosevelt and Prime Minister Churchill thought that the Russians had gone back on their word and were foisting a Communist regime on Poland. When President Truman came into office he gave a dressing-down to the Soviet foreign minister and told him that Stalin was not living up to his word.

Stalin didn't take this lying down, and the correspondence on this subject, which went on just as victory was being achieved in Europe, was extraordinary for the language used by allies toward each other. Stalin even thought that the Western allies had made some kind of a deal with the Nazis behind his back, which supposedly accounted for the rapid advance of the Western allies into Germany. Hardly was the war over when the Russians made territorial demands on neutral Turkey and sponsored breakaway regimes in two northwestern provinces of Iran. Later there was added the issue of Russian-sponsored takeovers of power in Romania, Bulgaria and Hungary. In 1946 the Communists rose up in Greece and conducted a three-year civil war in which they received vital support and sanctuary from three Communist countries across the border.

A wave of fear swept over Western Europe as a result of the "cold" takeover of the government of Czechoslovakia by the Communists in 1948 and of the Soviet blockade of West Berlin, which was designed to squeeze the Western allies out of the erstwhile German capital. I have already mentioned the shock and dismay that the invasion of South Korea in 1950 caused in the West, not only in the United States (and also of course in Japan) but especially in Western Europe.

It is this succession of shocks at the hands of the Russians that accounted for the feeling in the West that if we were to avoid another big war, and if we were to apply the lessons learned from the events that had led up to the last one, we would have to block Soviet expansion by a policy of "containment." That policy sought to avoid open conflict by making it clear to the Russians, and later to the Chinese as well, that the West, and first and foremost the United States, would not brook any further expansion of their empire. (At the same time we gave conclusive evidence in 1956, when we failed to intervene in the Hungarian uprising, that we did not expect to roll back Russian power.) The purpose of our policy was essentially defensive in the face of what we saw as an expansive Communist monolith. The Russians very likely saw containment as something else, and began to speak of capitalist imperialist efforts to "encircle" them.

The fact that China had been taken over by the Communists in 1949 was attributed by the opposition in the U.S. to stupidity or even treason in high places in the U.S. Government. The United States was said to have "lost" China, as if it had belonged to us. Those were the days of what the historian D.W. Brogan has called "the myth of American omnipotence," when we thought that we could do anything, and if we failed it could only be because we had just not gone about it the right way. We also believed that we had a duty to help people everywhere who were threatened by Communist aggression or foreign-supported subversion. So we could not imagine that, if we put our mind to it, we couldn't prevent South Vietnam from being taken over by men in black pajamas whose footgear was often made of old automobile tires.

I think this is a fair rendition of the attitudes not only of our government but also of most of our people toward intervention in Vietnam, which became really important only in the mid-1960s. We wanted nothing for ourselves in Southeast Asia. Although the Vietnamese Communists pictured us as the successors of the French colonialists, we saw our role as entirely different because we just wanted to assure the continued existence of a viable, independent South Vietnam. There was a certain plausibility to what we were trying to do because we had already prevented one part of another divided country, Korea, from swallowing up the other, and we were determined to prevent one part of Vietnam from swallowing up the other.

"Wars of National Liberation"

In this situation there supervened an event which was to have momentous consequences on American thinking about Vietnam. Just after the election of 1960 which brought John F. Kennedy into the White House but still before the inauguration, on January 6, 1961 to be exact, Nikita Khrushchev, First Secretary of the Communist Party of the Soviet Union, made an important speech in Moscow. He bragged that the Soviet Union was now so powerful that it could prevent the "imperialists" from starting a war, and at the same time spoke warmly about "wars of national liberation," which he said were just wars and necessary wars. The Communists, he said, do not export revolution. But if there are revolutions in the present or former colonial territories, then it is the duty of socialist (meaning Communist) countries to support those revolutions and wars of national liberation. It is absolutely inadmissible, however, for the imperialists to "export counterrevolution" by supporting any of the governments that are thus attacked by forces of national liberation; and Khrushchev cited Cuba, Algeria and Vietnamas examples of "wars of national liberation" that deserved full Communist support.

I remember the Khrushchev speech of January 1961 especially vividly because at the time I was working in the Bureau of African Affairs in the State Department, and the Executive Secretary of the Department, Lucius Battle, sent a copy of the Khrushchev speech to every policy officer with a memorandum stating that the Secretary of State, Dean Rusk, wanted all of us to read it in its entirety. The Khrushchev speech and the theme of "wars of national liberation" were perceived as a direct challenge to the containment policy of the United States.

As I see it, the new Communist emphasis was in fact a kind of tribute to the efficacy of containment. Unable to expand directly anywhere along their perimeter, the Russians now proposed to help revolutions far away from their shores by in effect leaping over the wall that the containment policy had erected around them. Counterinsurgency, counterguerrilla, unconventional war, limited war, now became the watchwords of the new Kennedy Administration. Kennedy had criticized his predecessor Eisenhower for excessive reliance on nuclear retaliation and had warned that we were not adequately prepared to fight small conventional "brushfire" wars in faraway places.

The Khrushchev speech and the Communist-instigated attack against the government of South Vietnam now seemed to prove the validity of Kennedy's campaign slogans. An entire new military discipline was developed out of counterinsurgency. State Department officers, too, had to go to special training courses in counterinsurgency. Vietnam seemed an excellent place for our military to apply what they were just learning, and successful work in counterinsurgency seemed a promising means for obtaining advancement in one's military career. The U.S. military thought they were ready and able to cope with "insurgency" in South Vietnam.

North Vietnam Starts Second Round

The first phase of the Second Indochina War (the one in which the United States participated) was a guerrilla war begun by the remaining Viet Minh (now called Viet Cong) in the south, and supplemented by other Communist guerrillas who were infiltrated from the north. For a long time there was a lot of controversy over whether this was an authentic South Vietnamese insurrection or a foreign-instigated and supported civil war that could be termed a form of aggression by North Vietnam against the South. This is now pretty well settled because after they won the war the North Vietnamese published their own history of it and for the first time acknowledged what they had previously denied, that the North Vietnamese Communist party, the Lao Dong Party, formally decided in 1959 to start a military campaign to bring about the overthrow of the government of Ngo Dinh Diem.

The infiltrations began in 1960 when trained former Viet Minh who had been taken to the North after the Geneva Agreement were being sent back to the South. So I think it is fair to say that we have a sort of continuum. In the beginning there was an uprising of South Vietnamese Communists in South Vietnam, even though the signal for it and the direction and supply came from the North. Then the North sent additional people, first southerners trained in the North and then northerners, and later the North sent full military divisions; and of course at the very end, in 1975 when they won the war, the North Vietnamese had fully equipped modern armored and mechanized infantry divisions in the South and were conducting a conventional military invasion.

I don't want to burden you with a lot of dates, but for this phase of the war it is important to note that it was 1959 when the decision was made in Hanoi; 1960 when the first major infiltrations began; 1963 when Diem was overthrown and assassinated; 1964 when the Congress passed a resolution authorizing military action in Southeast Asia; and 1965 when the United States sent fully equipped combat troops into Vietnam.

President Kennedy first sent only advisors. The first was killed in 1959 by a bomb that was thrown in a movie house. By the time Kennedy died we had 10,000 military advisors in Vietnam. I think it must be clear that not all those 10,000 soldiers gave advice. When the United States sends military personnel into a foreign country, particularly a developing country, they don't come alone; they bring along a tremendous amount of paraphernalia, from air-conditioning for their barracks to PX's and post offices and xerox machines and electric typewriters plus their own power generators—in short, the so-called "logistic tail'' for which the Americans are famous and which provides a remarkable stimulus to the economy of any country to which we send our military. Even just 10,000 American advisors were quite a conspicuous presence.

The British in World War II used to complain about the Americans that they were "overfed, overpaid, oversexed, and over here." I'm using the British parallel deliberately, for I don't for a moment think that the Americans were unpopular in Vietnam, any more than they were in England. By and large the South Vietnamese were glad to have them, but the presence of foreigners throwing money around and wanting female companionship and enjoying such a manifestly high standard of living is bound to create problems in an environment in which the people belong to a different culture and live on a very different footing. Later, when American firepower was used in Vietnam, naturally those who were at the receiving end of it could not have been very happy about the Americans who sometimes burned the house down in order to get at the rats. But by and large the Americans were not unpopular.

Reflections on Guerrilla Warfare

I have mentioned guerrilla warfare as having started in 1960, and this is a term that is not easily understood, especially in the situation of Vietnam. Mao Zedong, the Chinese Communist leader, once enunciated the dictum that guerrillas are like fish and the population among whom they move are like water—with the implication that if the people were not friendly to the guerrillas and supporting them and helping them, then the guerrillas could not move around freely and thus would not be effective. I would like to try to knock this idea firmly on the head because I think it has been thoroughly disproved in the case of Vietnam.

First of all I will ask you to make a leap of the imagination and picture yourselves living in a small village in South Vietnam, minding your own business and hoping to stay out of political conflicts. One day in the morning the school teacher of your village is found with his throat slit. He was universally liked and quite unpolitical, and there seems no reason why he should have been killed except that perhaps he might have refused to do something that was asked of him. Then you learn that the wife and children of the local policeman have been knifed to death during a night when the policeman was away. Still there is no sign of any guerrillas.

Then one night you hear a knock on your door. You open and two men come in carrying a wounded comrade, and they are Viet Cong and they ask if you could hide their comrade from the authorities and care for him until they can come and pick him up again. What would you do? Would you say no, you don't want to have anything to do with either the government or the VC? The Communists have just demonstrated that they will kill without compunction anyone who refuses to cooperate. And when they next come and "invite" you along to an indoctrination session, and when they later start demanding a "tax" from you, you go along And when government troops come to the village and ask if

28

you have seen any VC, would you say yes or would you find it prudent to keep your mouth shut like everyone else?

My point is that it is entirely possible for guerrillas to "swim in the sea" of a rural population that is not in sympathy with them at all if the guerrillas are utterly ruthless and if the government is not able to send soldiers to the villages who will stay there. Some of the villagers of course were in sympathy with the VC, and there were even fanatical, convinced Communists among them. But it is a very long jump from the fact that villagers often said that they had heard and seen nothing of the guerrillas, to the conclusion that the VC enjoyed widespread support. They were widely feared, yes, especially as long as government soldiers only came through on patrols and weren't yet able to protect the villagers.

Viet Cong Guerrilla Tactics

Far from being a spontaneous uprising of nationalist freedom fighters against an oppressive government, the guerrilla war started by North Vietnam in 1960 against the South Vietnamese government was in fact mostly directed against the South Vietnamese population. I know this is a controversial statement but it is very easily substantiated by looking at the statistics of Viet Cong terror practiced against the civil population. They resorted not only to continuous assassinations and kidnappings but to indiscriminate acts of terror, such as the mining of heavily traveled roads or the throwing of bombs into marketplaces and movie houses.

In other guerrilla wars, like the war in Spain against Napoleon or in Russia against the Nazis, the guerrillas hid in the mountains and in the forests and in whatever cover and concealment they could find in the countryside; but they did not establish fortified points in villages. In Vietnam, however, that is exactly what the VC did; and when government troops and later American troops were fired upon from such a village, they returned the fire, usually with overwhelming force, and the village was destroyed, and new refugees were generated. The "generating" of refugees was a deliberate tactic of the VC

I was asked sometimes why it took so many soldiers to control just a few thousand guerrillas, for in the beginning the war involved only perhaps between 10,000 and 20,000 Viet Cong and perhaps ten times as many government soldiers. To answer that question I would ask you to make another leap of the imagination and think what it would be like right here in Georgetown if a mad arsonist were on the loose. He would go into some back alley and pour gasoline and set a house on fire, and by the time people noticed he would be gone. Now imagine that your arsonist works as part of a team with early reconnaissance and a getaway car and with everyone having a pre-rehearsed role to play. Such a team would be pretty hard to catch. But now imagine there is not just one such group but perhaps *twenty-five* groups of arsonists here in Georgetown, making altogether $25 \times 3 = 75$ people.

And now imagine further that there are ten other areas in the District of

29

Columbia where you also have 25 groups each preparing and executing arson attacks, a total of 250 arson teams of altogether 750 people. Seven hundred fifty out of a population of 750,000 is one-tenth of one percent. That is all it would take to create utter pandemonium in our city. How many fire fighters and how many police would you need to cope with that many arsonists? Would it be 750 or something more like ten or twenty times as many?

The fact is that when the objective of the guerrilla is only to kill and destroy and not to build and maintain, he has an enormous advantage over the government, which must try to guard and prevent and protect and anticipate and respond and pursue. Perhaps if we had 750 arsonists in Washington some observers abroad would conclude that "the people" were rising up against an unpopular American government, but terrorism is never a reliable indicator of the state of public opinion. Actually it was a measure of their unpopularity that the Viet Cong in South Vietnam never managed to paralyze a city or even a major town with terrorism. And when they came into the cities in force during the spring holiday of Tet 1968, they found that the population turned against them, gave them no succor and immediately denounced them to the authorities—except for Hué, which was overrun and held for six weeks by North Vietnamese regulars, during which period they systematically murdered over three thousand civilians.

Kennedy's Fundamental Choice

Soon after President Kennedy came into office the problem had to be faced that things were not going well in South Vietnam. The guerrilla warfare against the government was increasing, the army which had been trained to fend off a conventional offensive from North Vietnam across the Demilitarized Zone in the north was performing poorly, and the question was whether the United States might not be better off if it washed its hands of the whole business. A number of possible options were discussed between the President and his National Security Adviser, Walt W. Rostow, and the following conclusion was reached by the President, as reported by Rostow:

> He began with domestic political life. He said if we walked away from Southeast Asia, the communist takeover would produce a debate in the United States more acute than that over the loss of China. Unlike Truman with China or Eisenhower in 1954, he would be violating a treaty commitment to the area. The upshot would be a rise and convergence of left- and right-wing isolationism that would affect commitments in Europe as well as in Asia. Loss of confidence in the United States would be worldwide. Under these circumstances, Khrushchev and Mao could not refrain from acting to exploit the apparent shift in the balance of power. If Burma fell, Chinese power would be on the Indian frontier; the stability of all Asia, not merely Southeast Asia, was involved. When the communist leaders had moved— after they were committed—the United States would then react. We would

come plunging back to retrieve the situation. And a much more dangerous crisis would result, quite possibly a nuclear crisis.

In other words, the President felt the people of the United States would not stand for a Communist takeover of South Vietnam. This has been sometimes interpreted as meaning that the President began our commitment to the defense of South Vietnam for "domestic political reasons," but that in my opinion is a mixed-up way of looking at the American political process. When President Kennedy decided to face down the Russians during the Cuban Missile Crisis, he remarked to his brother that he thought he would have been impeached if he had failed to act. In other words, he was leading a nation that wanted to be led where he was taking it. In the same way Kennedy's attitude toward Vietnam really represented the mainstream of American opinion, which has continued to this day to be in favor of containing the

John F. Kennedy

power of the Soviet Union and China. At times we have been unaware that containment was what we and our allies were trying to accomplish, and at times we failed in our efforts to contain; but Kennedy's decision to commit the United States, and Johnson's later decision to send in the troops, and Nixon's later decision not to leave our South Vietnamese ally in the lurch were all of one piece.

If you are an opponent of the war you can say that the mistake was inevitable in view of what preceded it. But that is true of all the actions of people and of nations—they are the product of what preceded them. Many people thought we were fighting a weak and small Southeast Asian country, but actually our commitment in Southeast Asia was matched by the logistic might of the Soviet Union. Whatever we bombed, over the years, in North Vietnam or South Vietnam or Laos or Cambodia was diligently replaced by the USSR and even increased. What seemed a war on the periphery that we were bound to win turned out to be an integral part of the Cold War on ideologically very unfortunate terms, because we were fighting a fanatical and disciplined enemy who had combined the appeals of nationalism and egalitarianism—among the most powerful political appeals to human hearts and minds that have ever existed—and used them against us with the material support of the other superpower.

The Rostow Mission

Having decided that the costs of failing to hold Southeast Asia outweighed the burden of meeting the challenge, Kennedy still had to decide just how to meet that challenge—whether to go directly to the source of aggression or to strengthen the hands of those under attack. But the most fundamental question in Kennedy's mind, as reported by Rostow, was this: Did the people of South Vietnam really

31

want an independent non-Communist future or did they in fact prefer to go with Ho Chi Minh and Hanoi? The President instructed Rostow to go to Vietnam, where Frederic Nolting was then the American Ambassador. With the help of our embassy Rostow took up first-hand contact with exponents of the government and especially with exponents of the various factions of the opposition, to get a picture of what it was that the South Vietnamese wanted.

There was no dearth of oppositionists to talk to in Saigon. The city was teeming with disappointed politicians, former office holders who had been removed by Diem, and ambitious candidates for the succession. There were also many idealistic oppositionists and especially people who chafed under the semi-authoritarian regime, which gave little freedom of expression. All these people were readily available to foreigners and in fact maintained a kind of cottage industry of keeping foreign embassies and media people supplied with derogatory information about their government. Rostow wrote in his book *The Diffusion of Power:*

> I listened to their complaints, with which Saigon was full. I then would ask: Do you wish a unified Vietnam under Hanoi? The prompt and universal answer was negative. I then probed at why they held such a negative view. They were often surprised that I put the question with evident seriousness. The tone of the conversation changed from colorful efforts to lobby an American official on Diem's deficiencies to quiet reflection. They described in detail what had happened in the north between 1954 and 1956; the changed view of Ho Chi Minh as the refugees came and reported their experiences . . . Then I probed at attitudes in the hamlets and villages and small towns. There, of course, the concerns were primarily local. As in almost all developing nations, central government was regarded as a distant instrument taking away sons and money. The army was as much an intruder as a protector, making off with chickens and rice. They wished to be left alone to raise their food in peace and enjoy the round of family and village life. The communists were feared. They, too, laid claim on sons and rice—plus intelligence on the movement of government forces.

All right, I think you get the idea. I have tried to build up, piece by piece, the underlying situation of the early part of the Second Indochina War: The difference between North and South, the nature of the terrain and the opportunity for concealment that it offers, the impossibility of interdicting the Communist infiltration which came not only across the demilitarized zone but also across the border between South Vietnam and Laos and later across the border between South Vietnam and Cambodia; the terrorist nature of the guerrillas in the countryside; the weakness of the VC in the cities; the tremendous advantage that guerrillas have against any government when their purpose is just to make life miserable for the people. I have sketched out the American government's attitude toward helping Vietnam and the reasons behind it. But I cannot any longer delay talking about another factor, the weaknesses of our South Vietnamese ally.

Decline and Fall of Ngo Dinh Diem

About the position and performance of Ngo Dinh Diem, I have quoted from a report that correctly described him as autocratic and stubborn. He was also quite ineffective in the pursuit of the war against the guerrillas. He had first tried to expand the South Vietnamese army, but without a counterguerrilla doctrine they just blundered about looking for set-piece battles that never took place. He also began to concentrate the rural population in so-called strategic hamlets which were lightly fortified and defended for the most part by the peasants themselves. The program had some limited success, but often the peasants regarded those hamlets more as concentration camps than as living places, particularly since of necessity they had to be placed away, and sometimes very far away, from the fields of the peasants.

I cannot go into much detail about Diem. He became more and more unpopular in America. He locked up political rivals and enemies. There was corruption in his immediate entourage, and he got into an embarrassing conflict with the Buddhists, especially in the city of Hué and at the Xa Loi pagoda in Saigon. The Buddhists then claimed to be persecuted by the government which was, after all, led by a Catholic. The claim seemed all the more plausible when some of the Buddhist monks protested against the alleged oppression by publicly pouring gasoline over themselves and setting themselves on fire.

Somehow this demonstration of the seriousness of some of these Buddhist monks was taken as evidence of the justness of their complaints—a fallacy that one is naturally prone to; but just because somebody is willing to sacrifice his life does not by any means prove that the cause for which he is willing to make that sacrifice is just and right. Actually the Buddhist demonstrations against the government were not representative of the attitude of the Buddhist population as a whole. The government made a number of concessions to the Xa Loi pagoda bonzes, but each led to further demands; and it turned out that the Buddhist demonstrations were the work of some politically ambitious monks and not a religious matter at all. But the American press, which was already down on Diem because of his autocratic style of government, the corruption, and the inefficiency of his defense against the VC, fastened on the Buddhist disorders of 1961 and 1962 as evidence that South Vietnam was coming apart and that it was impossible for us to save the country unless we managed to get rid of Diem. And that is precisely what we did.

We did not directly instigate the coup against Diem, but we gave a clear signal that a coup would not be unwelcome when President Kennedy in 1963 publicly criticized the regime in Saigon and broadly implied that it would be difficult for us to help South Vietnam effectively under the prevailing circumstances. And so Diem was overthrown by the Vietnamese military. We were shocked when he was killed and dismayed when the generals who then took over were no more democratic and no more effective than he had been, had the same troubles with the Buddhist militants, and thus did not bring greater stability to South Vietnam.

33

As a French proverb has it, one must want also the consequences of what one wants. When there is a coup in a foreign country you cannot fine-tune what then happens. You cannot usually predict who will come out on top, and you cannot, certainly, prescribe the manner in which the new government will govern (unless you take over completely as the Russians did in Afghanistan).

We got rid of Diem, but the situation deteriorated further. Diem's organization in the countryside came apart; the North Vietnamese pushed more men into South Vietnam; the South Vietnamese military continued to flounder in their efforts to control the guerrillas; and President Kennedy was once more confronted with the choice of increasing the American effort of support or cutting it and getting out. Not long after that he was himself assassinated.

Role of the Mass Media

I would like to pause here for a moment and discuss with you the role that the American media played in the downfall of Ngo Dinh Diem and how certain patterns emerged which were to bedevil the American effort in Vietnam throughout the time we were there. In order to make my point I will seemingly digress and tell you the story of something I experienced during World War II when I was in psychological warfare and we sent a team along to give propaganda support to the American landing at Casablanca in November 1942. We had a French radio announcer who was to broadcast from an American battleship on the same wavelength as Radio Casablanca, telling the French military there that we were coming as friends, that we wanted to liberate France and that they should not oppose our landing. We also sent a French-speaking American journalist along, a gentleman by the name of Winner, and I vividly remember his report about the operation when he returned to Washington.

He said it had been an utter disaster. Nothing had gone right. The radio broadcast must have been on the wrong wavelength for nobody in Casablanca had heard it. Some of our landing craft capsized upon launching. Others encountered underwater obstacles that had not been reported by the reconnaissance. Some of the naval gunfire almost fell on our own troops. "The whole thing," said Mr. Winner, "reminded me of a gigantic train wreck." (I want to emphasize that across a distance of over forty years I do not really remember the details of what Winner reported, just the general tenor and the fact that he had *much substantiating detail*.) Yet our landing at Casablanca was a success, it achieved all its objectives, the French did not oppose us, and we got all our troops on land even though there were some mishaps as there always are in large and complex military operations.

It occurred to me then, as I imagine it must also have occurred to you now, that while everything that Winner reported was true, he had *observed selectively*. Somehow he had managed to miss that he was present at an operation that was basically a success. He missed that because he was a keen and critical observer of all the things that went wrong. He was trained that way. The successful landing of five thousand men was to him not the story—the story was the confusion and mix-ups and failures and disappointments and misunderstandings and deficiencies that were revealed in the operation. He told *his* story, but it wasn't the story that really mattered. Of course if he had tried to file from Casablanca a story along the lines of his report to us, he would have been prevented from doing so by censorship. There was no freedom of reporting in World War II—indeed there hasn't been such freedom in any war in history until the Vietnam War.

In all wars except the Vietnam War the government decided that reporting on the seamy side of what they were doing, on the failures and shortcomings and mistakes and the cruelty and suffering of war and the innocent victims and the occasional cases of cowardice or dishonesty— none of these things could be reported; but in Vietnam the press made a specialty of them—and certainly the government of Ngo Dinh Diem offered plentiful material for reporting on the weaknesses and failures and scandals and opposition criticisms of our South Vietnamese ally. For as we have seen from the experiences there of Dr. Rostow, there was a vocal opposition in Saigon because Diem ran a loose authoritarian regime and not a tight totalitarian one like that of Ho Chi Minh in the North.

I would say with no exaggeration that Diem was essentially done in by the American press. One year after his ouster and death the Pulitzer Prize for International Reporting went to the two journalists who had most distinguished themselves by keeping up a drumfire of denunciatory reporting about Diem's weaknesses and iniquities, namely David Halberstam of the *New York Times* and Malcolm W. Browne of the Associated Press. Halberstam had even acknowledged to several people that he considered it his foremost purpose in Vietnam to "get" Diem. Well, he got him.

Washington Believes the Media

The Buddhists of the Xa Loi pagoda played the American press like one plays a piano. Demonstrations were carefully arranged for maximum media play. For instance, television cameras were ready and in place when monks appeared who were going to immolate themselves by pouring gasoline over themselves. Later a Buddhist press flack with shaved head and saffron robe called the Venerable Thich Duc Nhiep (all bonzes were called "venerable") would inquire from reporters about "the play" that the carefully staged events had received in Washington and New York. Marguerite Higgins reported in her book *Our Vietnam Nightmare:*

> To the observant riot watcher the demonstrations were obviously stage-managed with a view to provoking violence. The professional touch is always apparent when the 'riot managers' put women and children in front, then use them as a shield. Standing behind this human shield, the demonstrators start throwing things—rocks, bits of metal, etc.—at the police. So when

35

the police retaliate they have to wade first through the women and children. This provides a dramatic shot for the photographers—this picture of uniformed police plowing through innocent-looking women and children to get at the rock-throwing. I was to see the same stage-managed riots over and over again in the next two years in Vietnam, often with the same veteran riot leaders in command as in the Diem days.

Wide World Photos

Famous 1963 Photograph

Of course, when we are talking here of the electronic media this means first and foremost the television news, which has a peculiar predilection for the dramatic shot covered with "voice over" comment, usually ending with a so-called "stand up" commentary by the reporter, who must transform himself into a commentator trying to draw some conclusions of general validity from what has just been shown. So it is natural, perhaps, that reporters showing burning monks and other horrors of Vietnam tended to come into the American viewers' living rooms or bedrooms also with some portentous generalization of an ominously negative nature about what was happening in Vietnam.

Perhaps it was inevitable that more and more the difficulties that Diem was having with "the Buddhists" were seen as a reason why he could not pursue the war against the Communist guerrillas effectively. An Assistant Secretary of State who was sent out from Washington reported that the Buddhist crisis was having an effect on Vietnamese army morale. Challenged on this by the American Ambassador, who happened to be on consultation in Washington, the Assistant Secretary was asked if he based this information on the reporting of the *New York Times*. The answer of Assistant Secretary Roger Hillsman, according to Ambassador Frederick Nolting, was "Partly; I also based it on other wire dispatches from Saigon." Mr. Halberstam, the *New York Times* correspondent in Saigon, later denied that he had pictured the Buddhist demonstrations as a religious crisis. But his colleague Higgins, an old-time campaigner who had been through World War II, concluded in her book, *Our Vietnam Nightmare*, that "whatever Mr. Halberstam's intentions, his and other press dispatches of the time did create the impression that some kind of religious crisis was going on."

The thing to retain here is that the press had become a major factor in the drama that was unfolding in Vietnam; that it tended to have its own point of view, sometimes single-mindedly committed to a particular purpose; and that already under Kennedy our government often believed the vivid reporting of the media more than it believed its own representatives on the spot. This is a pattern that we will encounter again, most importantly in connection with the Tet Offensive, which was probably the turning point of the Second Indochina War.

*Lecture Three*_____

AFTER THE LAST LECTURE I was asked if I think that the way our mass media reported and commented on the war accounts for the fact that we failed in Vietnam. Some of you had left by the time that question was asked, so I would like to repeat my answer. Please note that I am very careful in phrasing it. The answer is, "no" because I think it is vulgar and unscientific to assign determining importance to one single factor in a complex political and historical equation. Many factors accounted for the fact that we lost the war in Vietnam. But among them certainly the emergence of high-speed telecommunications including the rapid transmission of still pictures and moving pictures was significant, raising an entirely new question about our ability to win any future war, except perhaps a very short one. In other words, I recognize that the way the electronic media reported it was an exceedingly important factor in the outcome of the war, because the American public and Congress and even the White House often gave more credence to the presentation of facts and their interpretation by the media than to the reports of the official representatives on the spot.

I don't mean to say that those official representatives were always right or that the media were always wrong. That would be silly. What I will explain in detail, in this lecture and in the final one, is that some of the most powerful electronic media do not lend themselves well to *explaining* things; that it is entirely possible to report truthfully but to mislead the reader or viewer because of the selectiveness with which one portion of the truth is sought or perceived or conveyed; and yes, at certain critical junctures I believe it can be demonstrated that the way in which the media reported and interpreted news from Vietnam had a direct effect on policy decisions, some of them questionable ones. I have already cited one such instance in connection with the conflict between the Diem government and the Buddhists of Xa Loi pagoda and how at least one influential American journalist had seen it as his purpose to "get" the head of state of a friendly country.

Backing into the War

In August 1964 two American destroyers on patrol in international waters in the Gulf of Tonkin, off the coast of North Vietnam, were fired upon by North Vietnamese torpedo boats. President Johnson immediately ordered retaliatory air strikes against North Vietnamese shore installations and went to Congress asking for authority to respond to aggression in Southeast Asia. The resolution was quite sweeping and it was passed with little debate, by 88 to 2 in the Senate and 416 to 0 in the House.

Later it turned out that the South Vietnamese Navy had been conducting a secret operation against North Vietnam in the vicinity and that the North Vietnamese attack could have been on the plausible assumption that the American destroyers were involved in that operation. The Tonkin Gulf resolution was

Lyndon B. Johnson

accordingly perceived as the result of a deception on the part of our government, and six years later, when the war had become very unpopular, the Congress repealed the resolution. I think there is little doubt that President Johnson seized on the incident in the Tonkin Gulf to obtain a congressional mandate for intervention, but historians are not certain that he had really decided to intervene before the elections in 1964. In the campaign Senator Goldwater advocated crushing North Vietnam, and President Johnson argued against American intervention.

Since a few months after the 1964 elections President Johnson ordered a massive bombing campaign against North Vietnam and by mid-1965 had sent a substantial military force, the view has been expressed that the President tricked the country by taking it into a war it did not want. Others take the position that the Congress knew perfectly well what it was doing in 1964 and that it was only when the war became drawn out and very costly and increasingly unpopular that Congress discovered that if it had had all the facts it would not have given President Johnson the resolution he wanted.

It seems to me that while the government was less than candid with the Congress in the matter of the Tonkin Gulf resolution, too much can be made of that aspect of how we got into the war: Just as President Wilson kept campaigning on the basis of promises to keep us out of World War I, then seized on pretexts to get us in at a time when it was obvious that sooner or later the United States was going to go in; just as President Franklin Roosevelt backed us into World War II, after making campaign promises that he would not send American boys to die abroad, at a time when everybody realized that American entry into World War II was inevitable; so President Johnson in my opinion also backed us into the Vietnam War, by pretexts and subterfuges, at a time when Congress was certainly willing to have us do what needed to be done to keep South Vietnam from being taken over by the North Vietnamese Communists.

The decisions that got the United States into full-fledged war in Vietnam were taken over a period of time. They are among the most analyzed decisions of any American government, partly because the ten-volume Pentagon Papers in 1971 revealed everything that the Defense Department knew about high-level decision making, and partly because some of the participants have written books about the matter, as did academics and journalists. The question usually is: How could it be that the United States with all the copious intelligence it possessed about the situation and with such brilliant and sophisticated advisers around the President—how could we have "blundered" into such a "quagmire"?

There is one school of thought that attributes the virtual unanimity in the top counsels of the White House at the various steps of intervention to something called "group think." The idea seems to be that when a number of top executives are caught in the vortex of fast-moving events and things go badly and they come in for criticism and are confronted with increasingly awful dilemmas, they tend to close ranks and mutually reinforce each other and close their minds to outside advice. This hypothesis seems to me rather farfetched. The President had access to contrary opinion, but those who expressed it *could not plausibly demonstrate that the consequences of leaving South Vietnam in the lurch would not be worse for the United States than the consequences of increasing the American commitment.*

Early Opponents of Intervention

In particular I call your attention to two viewpoints that deserve close attention. In one case the person who opposed our entry into the war was a high-ranking member of the inner circle around President Johnson, namely Undersecretary of State George Ball, who is now something of an elder statesman; and I will detail to you also the view of Leslie Gelb, because his analysis of how we got in deeper and deeper is very thought-provoking. George Ball's repeated memoranda to President Johnson—first against our involvement and then advocating that we cut our commitments and get out of Indochina—are impressive evidence that dissent was not stifled within the upper reaches of the government. But an analysis of the memoranda shows that while Ball was very precise in arguing that the war could not be won, he was less than precise when he advocated what we should do. He did not say that we should accept defeat but only that we should seek some kind of "compromise" with the enemy.

The idea that North Vietnam would be willing to compromise, if only the United States were more flexible and reasonable, was assiduously promoted by opponents of the war, but it has absolutely no support from any evidence whatsoever. In fact all the evidence is in the other direction. The North Vietnamese wanted it all—they weren't prepared to settle for less.

In the same category of dissent as Mr. Ball are the people, including some in Congress, who proposed that we should "declare victory and get out." But no juggling with words would have made out of unilateral withdrawal anything other than a humiliating acceptance of defeat and a betrayal of the South Vietnamese. My friend Paul Kattenberg, a Foreign Service officer, has been admired for telling a meeting of the National Security Council that he thought we should "consider withdrawal with honor." The idea was coolly received, I think, not because the group had closed its mind but because nobody then or since has been able to explain how leaving the South Vietnamese in the lurch could have been viewed by the people of America and the world as anything in the slightest honorable.

The trouble with such proposals was that they did not say clearly: "If we pull out we will have to pay a heavy price in terms of world confidence in our commitments, in terms of Communist respect for our power, and in terms of danger to other neighbors of Communist states, but I recommend that we pay that price." During the period when the American commitment was gradually increased, few people were that forthright in opposing the American effort to defend South Vietnam. George Kennan, the diplomat-historian who coined the term "containment," testified before a House committee in 1965 that we had no business in Vietnam and that we should disengage from there. He was asked: Would this not mean abdicating our role in Asia and handing a victory to the Communists? "I hope there is no misunderstanding," Kennan replied. "I am not advocating that we pick up and leave Vietnam." It is the intellectual poverty of such positions that astounds in retrospect, more than the fact that we gradually upped the commitment until in 1969 we had 541,000 men in Vietnam.

The view that I characterized as "thought-provoking" was expressed by Leslie H. Gelb and Richard K. Betts in their book, *The Irony of Vietnam: The System Worked*. The authors are of the opinion that the reason the top policymakers in the United States made the "wrong" decisions and got us deeper and deeper into the war was that they all shared the same mistaken set of ideas about the need to oppose Communist expansion, a basic premise that they attribute to dogmatism and ideological thinking:

> If Vietnam were a story of how the decision-making system failed, that is, a story of how U.S. leaders did not do what they wanted to do, did not realize what they were doing, did not understand what was happening, or got their way principally by lying to Congress and the American people, it would be easy to package a large and assorted box of panaceas. There are many examples . . . fix the way progress is measured in a guerrilla war; improve the analysis of intelligence; concentrate more on the political and economic dimensions of conflict and less on the military side; tell the American people more of the truth to prepare them for the sacrifices of the long haul; make sure the President sees the real alternatives; involve Congress more; and so forth. These are interesting and some are of consequence, but it is the thesis of this book that improvements in any of these respects would not have appreciably altered the thrust of the war . . . because the United States political-bureaucratic system did not fail; it worked.

So in the view of those critics our alleged mistakes in Vietnam were inevitable because our underlying assumption was not questioned. The real trouble was that a consensus existed on containing Communism. If the President had been more candid with the Congress or if more emphasis had been placed on social and economic change in South Vietnam, nothing material would have been different because the decision-making mechanism assumed that the overriding concern of the United States should be the containment of Communism.

I find this criticism illuminating and I hope you do, too. There is indeed a remarkable continuity in American foreign policy, and that continuity is due to the fact that nobody has come up with anything better or more plausible than the doctrine of containment. It is hard to see how our country would have been better served by what Gelb and Betts seem to advocate, a set of ad hoc policies devoid of any guiding principle or general understanding of what we are about.

As a matter of fact, the consensus that Gelb and Betts decried and which came apart as a result of Vietnam seems to be building up again, and I would regard that as a good thing. So in looking back I do not find it possible to blame Lyndon Johnson very much for having taken us into the Vietnam War. He got us in slowly and incrementally not necessarily to fool Congress or the American people, but because he hoped that every additional demonstration of American resolve would improve the chances for peace. In this of course he was mistaken.

Putting Pressure on Hanoi

In his memoirs Johnson described the reasoning behind the bombing campaign against North Vietnam that was started in 1965. "I hoped," he wrote, "that the leaders in Hanoi would read our messages carefully and understand their meaning. We were issuing no ultimatums that they might find impossible to accept, but it was important that they realize *they would pay a price* [emphasis added] if they continued to push their aggression to the south. There were limits to our long-demonstrated restraint and to self-imposed restrictions." But the North Vietnamese read the American message differently. They *decided to pay the price*, which seemed to them cheap. They correctly interpreted the great care we showed in the selection of targets to mean that we would not directly attack their cities, but in any case they evacuated many people. They did not have much industry; and they knew the Russians would help to replace what might be destroyed in the bombing.

As the Viet Cong were built up, equipped and organized, and established themselves in certain parts of South Vietnam, the size of their units increased and they were in a position to launch attacks on South Vietnamese outposts and even small population centers. So the Vietnamense army tried to engage those Viet Cong units, which turned out to be a very frustrating and costly business. In an area where the VC were strong and established the population would not cooperate with the government troops, so the South Vietnamese units often fell into ambushes and were gradually ground down, even when they had the help of American advisers.

At first the U.S. Marines held just a perimeter around the port city of Danang; but pretty soon it became apparent that if they wanted to assure the security of that perimeter, they would have to be able to go outside to patrol aggressively and also to engage enemy troops before they could mass for an attack. This, in a very schematic form, was the dilemma that confronted the U.S. command when American troops arrived in sizeable numbers—a choice (and I am simplifying) between the strategies of "clear and hold" and "search and destroy." The latter was usually very costly both in terms of American and South Vietnamese losses and in terms of suffering of the civilian population. But in my opinion there never really was such a choice, because you can only hold what you have cleared of the enemy if you are prepared to go out and search and if possible destroy the units that threaten the pacified area.

The American military effort in Vietnam was characterized by its reliance on high technology. It seems difficult to credit this in retrospect, but throughout the war the U.S. Air Force used the most up-to-date, high-performance supersonic aircraft to give air support to ground operations even though there were no enemy planes within hundreds of miles. The enormous "logistic tail" has already been mentioned—for every American soldier actually looking for the enemy there were perhaps six or seven performing various supply and support and maintenance and headquarters operations. Helicopters and armored personnel carriers gave us superior mobility, but the enemy was usually concealed on the ground and needed to be rooted out by foot-slogging soldiers. The Viet Cong and North Vietnamese were tough, resourceful and crafty. Except in rare instances they avoided pitched battles but fought a war of ambushes and surprise attacks, of land mines and sharpened pungee sticks. The American army has many good qualities, but crafty and stealthy it is not.

There are two things that I would like you to retain from this discussion of the military aspects of the war up to Tet 1968: first, that the efforts to destroy the VC and the North Vietnamese army units in South Vietnam inflicted a lot of suffering on the civilian population and created something like 1.2 million refugees between late 1965 and mid-1967 alone; and second, that while there were no real battles in which one could say who won and who lost, over time the VC and North Vietnamese were gradually pushed away from the most densely inhabited areas and the control exercised by the South Vietnamese government gradually increased—but there was nothing dramatic to point to.

How It Looked on the Tube

This situation created a real problem for the reporters, especially those whose medium required visual images. One could get pictures of a Vietnamese village being bombed or shelled and one would see the dead and wounded and the refugees streaming away with their possessions. Such things have happened in all wars, that when troops are attacked from a village they fire back into that village—I have seen it many times in Italy and France and Belgium in World War II and nobody thought it reprehensible at that time; but the Vietnam War was different because it was all filmed and almost instantaneously flashed into the living rooms and bedrooms of American homes, accompanied by comments on the horror and futility of such actions, creating the impression not only of a frustrating, aimless, inconclusive war—even when our side was making slow, incremental, cumulative progress—but also of an unusually cruel and destructive war. Of course the cruelty of the other side could not be shown because they did not allow American cameramen to film them.

Under this heading, the public image aspects of the war, comes also the high technology aspect of the American effort. For instance, certain key infiltration

44

routes along the borders of South Vietnam were emptied of their population and declared to be "free-fire zones." Actually those areas were quite small, for instance along the Van Co Dong River near the Cambodian border, about half a mile on each side of it. The idea of interdicting such an area by firing or dropping bombs into it at any time of the day or night was not a particularly effective tactic, but it surely was impressive: when photographers showed the bomb and artillery craters, a moon-like landscape literally plowed up by crater upon crater, the television viewer may be excused if somehow he associated that desolate strip of land with all of South Vietnam.

I have myself met American peace activists who thought that *inhabited* areas of Vietnam had been declared free-fire zones. Of course they never were. One could fly in a helicopter for hours over South Vietnam and not see any bomb or artillery damage. But naturally the electronic media preferred to picture again and again the bomb and artillery craters in a narrow free-fire zone as somehow illustrative of the American dilemma, which was that despite all our technological superiority and the brute force of our instruments of destruction we could not prevent continued infiltration of Viet Cong and North Vietnamese and their arms and supplies into South Vietnam.

Aspects of the "High Tech" War

I do not have time to discuss the military aspects in any detail, and these lectures do not pretend to give a full understanding of the strategic and tactical problems of the war. But for what it is worth I will give you my own view that essentially we were done in by high technology; because in many cases it was inapplicable and in all cases it was extraordinarily expensive and not at all cost-effective, and almost always it made us look more cruel and destructive than we actually were.

Take for instance the charge that was so often heard that we dropped more bombs on little Vietnam than were dropped in all of World War II in Europe and Japan. The accusation is true although it applies to all of Indochina including Cambodia and Laos, but what was too often overlooked is that most of those bombs were dropped on triple-canopy jungle in an attempt to interdict the flow of supplies down the so-called Ho Chi Minh Trail just parallel to the border in Laos and Cambodia. It was a tremendous effort—I myself have seen long strings of burning trucks resulting from extraordinarily sophisticated bombing attacks involving all kinds of electronic gadgets—but as I have already remarked, that bombing did not really slow the traffic down the trail very much, because for every truck that we destroyed the Russians landed another one or perhaps two or three in North Vietnam. We were spending enormous amounts of money to destroy equipment that was very cheaply replaced.

Or take another aspect, defoliation. This was something that inflamed some elements of public opinion in the United States, when claims were made that the chemicals we were using to clear jungle growth and to prevent the VC from growing food in certain remote areas were having the result of poisoning Vietnamese peasants and creating genetic damage that would last for generations. The principal defoliant was a herbicide used in the United States long after the war, for instance to keep the right of way of railroads free from underbrush. In Vietnam it was not only a matter of underbrush but of keeping areas, for instance cleared strips along highways, from being covered again by the encroaching jungle. Wherever there were human habitations nearby, the effort was strictly controlled. But when the choice was either killing a lot of people by bombing or shelling an isolated area held by the VC, or dropping herbicides to compel people to leave (and thus save themselves) and deprive the VC of food and sustenance, the latter alternative was judged more humane and lifesaving. Perhaps the judgment was not always right, but often there was no choice if substantial loss of life was to be avoided. In war one often has to choose between several evils, and even the lesser evil is still awful.

Much was made of the ecological damage done to the mangroves along the river channel leading up to Saigon. But it was in those mangroves that VC had been hiding and firing rockets at ships that had to come up the river to supply the capital. Tears were shed for the crocodiles whose habitat was ruined by repeated defoliation of such mangroves, but in this case the lives of millions of people depended on killing the hardy swamp plants with all the rest of the intricate ecological system of which they were part. Amazingly, however, the mangroves eventually grew back. But the pictures once more created the impression of vast areas of desolation.

I am showing this photograph of a Vietnamese child running away from a burning village because it exemplifies what I have said about the difficulty of

Wide World Photos

Prize-Winning Photograph

reporting and interpreting a war like the Vietnam War through the electronic media. The picture was in some way regarded as paradigmatic—as an outstandingly clear and typical example that can stand for a whole category—in this case as an example of the horrors perpetrated by American napalm bombing. The picture was taken at a place called Trang Band during an enemy offensive when the North Vietnamese and Viet Cong troops were attacking the town and a South Vietnamese plane by mistake dropped napalm on a pagoda where many people had taken refuge. The result, as far as Western readers and viewers were concerned, was a picture that graphically showed *suffering inflicted not by the attackers but by the defenders.* Senator George McGovern referred to this photograph in a speech, saying that it was symbolic of the suffering inflicted "in the name of America."

So the picture of that little girl became etched into the consciousness of the

American TV viewer and magazine reader and of people all over the world, just as the picture of the burning monk had become etched into the minds of people as illustrative of religious persecution by the Diem regime. Once such pictures have entered people's consciousness one cannot rectify the impression—people are no longer interested in hearing that the Buddhist monks of Hué were totally unrepresentative or that the little girl was the victim of a military accident. Visual paradigms have been suggested, and once created in people's minds they persist. This was a very interesting feature of the reporting of the Vietnam War.

The "Tet" Offensive 1968

I will devote the rest of this lecture to an analysis of the Tet (Vietnamese New Year) offensive of January/March 1968 because it was in many respects the turning point of the war. It was in the aftermath of that offensive that President Johnson announced he would not seek reelection and that he unilaterally stopped the bombing of North Vietnam in an effort to get the North Vietnamese to the conference table. The offensive produced a terrible shock in the American people. It started with a conventional enemy offensive in the central highlands where an American force of Marines was besieged in an encampment near a place called Khe Sanh.

And then in the night on January 30 a force of nineteen VC sappers blew a hole in the wall around the American embassy in Saigon and assaulted the embassy itself. There were tremendous headlines in the U.S., "Viet Cong in the American Embassy." This event, together with the VC and North Vietnamese attacks on virtually all the cities of South Vietnam, produced an impression that the enemy was everywhere, that his strength and determination must have been underestimated, that the Communists could move wherever they liked in Vietnam despite our massive military presence, and that something therefore was gravely wrong in our entire military posture and the war simply could not be won.

The impression of disaster conveyed by the media representatives in Saigon was undoubtedly also a reaction against excessively optimistic statements that had been made by the American military authorities. In a sense the press felt that they had been misled, and some of them may have felt they were now getting even. Never excessively trusting of the generally upbeat American military briefings, they henceforth systematically disbelieved whatever the American military were saying. Did not the eruption of the VC into the very city of Saigon constitute living proof that our military had been out of touch with reality when they had claimed that the enemy was almost beaten?

The nineteen VC who had invaded the grounds of the American embassy never got into the building and all were killed within hours; and as far as the invasion of the city was concerned, the South Vietnamese troops fought surprisingly well and together with American forces inflicted terrible losses on the Communists. Clearly the enemy planners had expected that the VC and North Vietnamese would be greeted as liberators. They must have been shattered when they discovered that the population wanted no part of them and freely gave information about them to the South Vietnamese police and military. Amazingly the Communists had made no plans for retreat or withdrawal anywhere, and so they were decimated.

But all the while the media focussed on the event in the American embassy—it took quite a while before it was clear that the VC had not even gotten into the building—and interpreted the widespread enemy attacks as evidence of Communist strength, instead of understanding it for what it was, a desperate throw of the dice to impress American public opinion and thus influence American policy. Television newscasters termed the war "lost" because the rural areas through which the Communists had passed were now "under Communist control." Actually it turned out the VC had had to deplete their forces in the countryside in order to break into the cities; and as a result of the Tet offensive the government in the following year vastly extended its control in the countryside, because big stretches of formerly "insecure" areas no longer had any VC or had VC who were so weak that they stopped fighting.

A "Paradigmatic" Picture of the Offensive

Aside from the focus on the daring but completely unsuccessful attempt on the American embassy, which resulted in a mass of news stories and pictures, the most sensational picture of the Tet offensive, which again was taken as para-

Wide World Photos

Famous 1968 Photograph

digmatic, was this one showing the South Vietnamese police general Nguyen Van Loan shooting a VC officer. There is obviously no doubt that this shooting constituted a war crime, and there can be no excuse for it, although there is an explanation. The VC officer's unit had taken position in an apartment house and from there had taken a terrible toll of Vietnamese police trying to storm the building; and when the building was finally regained and the VC taken away, the officer had sneered that he was now a prisoner of war and therefore entitled to full protection. Technically he was not a prisoner of war because he was wearing civilian clothes, but that doesn't mean that the South Vietnamese general had any right to kill him.

I stress the importance of this picture because the big story should have been what the Communists were doing to Saigon, transforming it into a battlefield—and how they were being received by the populace. But the image that was left with the American people, and with the world public, was not one of Communist cruelty or of South Vietnamese fighting success, but of the *cruelty of our ally*. The victims of aggression, and not the attackers, were held up to public scorn.

48

I want you to understand that I have not selected these three pictures—the burning monk, the fleeing child and the shooting of the prisoner—because they happen to illustrate a point that I am making about the war. Not at all. These are the three pictures that for the American TV viewer and the newspaper and magazine reader seemed paradigmatic, standing for important truths about the war, while actually, as you understand by now, they all represented *exceptions*: Far from being paradigmatic they were entirely untypical of what went on in the war. Here is the cover of *Newsweek* magazine when the war was over in

1975, seven years later. What did the editors of *Newsweek* think of when they were looking for a way to illustrate what people had known and felt about the Vietnam war? The shooting of the prisoner, the fleeing child, and the burning monk.

As I mentioned in the last lecture, in Hué where the North Vietnamese eventually had to be dug out of the old part of the city in arduous fighting, they murdered over three thousand civilians during the time they held that city. But there were no American photographers present when the Communists marched the victims off with their hands tied behind their backs and later when they shot them in the nape of the neck. On the other hand, there were

Newsweek May, 1975

also no photographers present when an American infantry company ran berserk in the village of My Lai and killed a number of innocent women and children.

I suppose the reason why My Lai was endlessly analyzed and castigated and why the killing of more than three thousand innocent people in Hué attracted relatively little attention is that Americans are held to higher standards than other people. Yet it deserves to be stressed that in Hué the Communists were *carrying out policy*, whereas at My Lai the Americans *violated their own military rules* of engagement. But somehow the American media in Vietnam did not display zeal in the investigation of Communist cruelties and atrocities, which were systematic and a matter of policy, and instead fastened at great length on the occasional violations of the rules of war by ourselves and our allies.

You may think this a digression but I would like to share with you one of the finest pieces of writing to come out of the Vietnam War. Michael Herr was a newspaper correspondent at Khe Sanh, the Marine encampment in the highlands that was surrounded by Communist troops during the Tet offensive. As soon as the siege began the press immediately compared Khe Sanh with Dien Bien Phu, where the French had had their Waterloo in the First Indochina War; but the differences were enormous. Khe Sanh was supplied by air throughout the siege and had a large artillery superiority over the enemy. The defenders could call on a huge effort of the United States Air Force, including bombings by B52s, the eight-motored strategic bombers. Yet all the TV anchormen in the U.S. kept drawing ominous parallels with the disaster suffered by the French, and there

49

was an atmosphere of grim foreboding in the reporting from Khe Sanh. Here is a passage by Michael Herr, reproduced from his book, *Dispatches*. He was writing about the central highlands:

> Everything up there was spooky, and it would have been that way even if there had been no war. You were there in a place where you didn't belong, where things were glimpsed for which you would have to pay and where things went unglimpsed for which you would also have to pay, a place where they didn't play with the mystery but killed you straight off for trespassing. The towns had names that laid a quick, chilly touch on your bones—Kontum, Dak Mat Lop, Dak Roman Peng, Poli Klang, Buon Plech, Pleiku, Pleime, Plei Vi Drin. Just moving through those towns or being based somewhere above them spaced you out, and every time I'd have that vision of myself lying dead somewhere, it was always up there in the highlands. It was enough to make an American commander sink to his knees and plead, "Oh God, just once let it be our way. We have the strength, give us the terms!" Not even the Cav, with their style and courage and mobility were able to penetrate that abiding highland face. They killed a lot of communists, but that was all they did, because the number of communist dead meant nothing, changed nothing.

Now, I submit to you that this is extraordinarily powerful writing. It really grips you and sends a chill down your spine. At the same time I would note that to someone like Herr, who thought the war inherently unwinnable, just about nothing could convince him that he was really witnessing a major American victory. The "terms" for which an American commander was supposed to have prayed on his knees, those terms were exactly what we got at Khe Sanh. Actually about 10,000 North Vietnamese were killed as they massed for attacks on Khe Sanh (there never was a major coordinated infantry assault because they were all broken up by artillery and bombing), and on the American side there were 205 Marines killed. Now one can say, and I would agree, that 205 dead Marines is 205 too many, but when you inflict such tremendous losses on an enemy and when that enemy has set himself a task of overrunning your position and he doesn't even get up to the wire, then the way in which one normally would describe that situation would be as a victory. But the situation wasn't normal. It was very special, and by quoting from Herr's book I hope I have captured a little of that special quality that surrounded much of the reporting.

Consequences of Media Perceptions

So the Tet offensive of 1968, while objectively clearly a defeat for the North Vietnamese and Viet Cong, was subjectively perceived in the United States as a defeat for the United States and its South Vietnamese ally, and this had very important consequences. Not only was our side, and not the side of our enemies, shown in the most distasteful light, but the pictures of death and destruction, of refugees and civilian suffering—juxtaposed against the earlier optimistic claims that had been made about progress in the war—created a wave of revulsion and pessimism. It did not matter that the attacking force lost about onehalf of its effectives, that it was unable to take its objective of Khe Sanh and unable to hold anything it did take. It did not matter that in fact the countryside was now denuded of VC, nor did it matter that the revolutionary claims of the Communists, that the people were on their side, had just been totally discredited.

The offensive was seen as evidence that the enemy was strong, that the American people had been lied to, that our allies were no good, that the war was hopeless, and that in any case the game was not worth the candle. I do not share the explanation of the media performance given by Peter Braestrup, who found that the media in Saigon during the Tet offensive did not behave very differently from the way they usually behave during fast-moving events when they tend to get their facts wrong initially and jump to premature conclusions. It was the total unwillingness of the media to correct the very misimpression about the Tet offensive that they had created which seems to me more important than the initial reporting of it.

Don Oberdorfer of the *Washington Post* in his book *Tet!* concluded that the offensive represented a grievous setback for the attackers and particularly the VC. "Tens of thousands of the most dedicated and experienced fighters emerged from the jungles and forests of the countryside only to meet a deadly rain of fire and steel within the cities. The Viet Cong lost the best of a generation of resistance fighters, and after Tet increasing numbers of North Vietnamese had to be sent south to fill the ranks. The war became increasingly a conventional battle and less an insurgency. Because the people of the cities did not rise up against the foreigners and puppets at Tet—indeed, they gave little support to the attack force—the Communist claim to a moral and political authority in South Vietnam suffered a serious blow." Oberdorfer also notes that after Tet the Saigon regime nearly doubled its military strength from 670,000 to roughly 1,100,000 men, displaying more political will than the South had ever been able to muster before. Yet this journalist considers the Tet offensive to have been on balance a North Vietnamese and Viet Cong victory. Why?

> In the United States, the consequences were even graver. The Tet offensive shocked a citizenry which had been led to believe that success in Vietnam was just around the corner. Tet was the final blow to the sagging credibility of the Johnson administration and to the waning patience of the American people with this remote and inconclusive war.

He does not explain how it could have been that what was such an enemy defeat on the ground could have created such shock and despondency in the United States. He doesn't explain it because he would have to refer to the way the offensive was reported and interpreted. Braestrup, in his book *Big Story*, cites chapter and verse of the skepticism of the editors in New York who disbelieved reports from Saigon that tried to correct the erroneous first impressions.

In late 1968, as reported by Edward J. Epstein, a producer for NBC suggested to the news department that they commission a series showing that Tet had indeed been a decisive military victory for America and that the media had exaggerated greatly the view that it was a defeat for South Vietnam. After some consideration, Epstein reports, "the idea was rejected because, Northshield [the editor] said later, Tet 'was already established in the public's mind as a defeat, *and therefore it was an American defeat.'* " I guess he was right. In politics what has actually happened is often less important than what people think has happened.

Lecture Four

It is now 1968, just after the Tet offensive, and it will be helpful if we look at trends rather than events.

The *first trend* of course was the growing unpopularity of the war. This was not unusual. We Americans have a history of becoming disenchanted rather rapidly with any war in which we participate unless we are clearly winning. This was true of our Civil War when Lincoln had to clap defeatists into jail as "copperheads" when they began to advocate a compromise with the enemy. It was true, certainly, in the Korean War when the stalemate on the 38th parallel led to rapid disenchantment and damaging opposition attacks on the government. But most of the responsible leaders who wanted the U.S. to pull out of Vietnam still did not actually come out and advocate that we accept defeat. They advocated concessions in the negotiations, they were in favor of pulling back troops, they called for a coalition government in Saigon, but except for a radical fringe they did not overtly and explicitly favor leaving the South Vietnamese in the lurch.

The *second trend* was inflation. There can be no doubt that the unwillingness of Lyndon Johnson to cut back his domestic programs and especially his unwillingness to put the nation on a war footing, for instance by asking for additional taxes, had a great deal to do with the economic mess in which we still find ourselves today. This was related to Johnson's commitment to his program of the "Great Society" and a civilized reluctance to inflame American passions against an enemy whom we did not wish to destroy, whom we just wanted to keep from taking over South Vietnam.

The *third trend* was toward more and more protest on the campuses and elsewhere by people who were often not only against the war but also, either by extension or separately, against the prevailing system, against the values of their elders, against the social order, against the way our society is organized. I think this third trend had a sufficient life of its own that it should be listed separately from the growing unpopularity of the war. It wasn't the unpopularity of the war that split the Democratic Party in 1968 but the venomous, almost anarchic behavior of the protesters who discombobulated the entire left of the political spectrum in the United States. It is all very well to say that the radical left was only a small fraction of the opposition to the war. The radical left created such a malaise in the American society that it set up a backlash; and that backlash heavily contributed to the election of Richard Nixon in the 1968 elections.

Meanwhile the *fourth trend* was the growing strength of the South Vietnamese government and the increasing weakness of the VC. It is an irony of history that just as the South Vietnamese under Nguyen Van Thieu were rising up and standing tall and giving every evidence that they had turned the corner and were getting the upper hand, at that same time Americans became more and more convinced that the war could not be won.

Tribute to the Viet Cong

I think this is a good point to say something about the heroism of the VC. I have referred to the terror tactics that they employed and I think you suspect that I was not a great admirer of those who employed them. But there is no doubt that among them were many sincere patriots and convinced social revolutionaries and that they made tremendous sacrifices and fought with great tenacity and ingenuity: But the important fact is that the best among them, the most audacious and highly motivated, were now dead. They had been decimated by the U.S.-South Vietnamese campaign before Tet, and then they were almost wiped out during Tet. They built up their forces again, partly by forced recruitment in the countryside, but from 1968 onward the war became one essentially between the North Vietnamese army and the South Vietnamese army. The very idea that the North had to send "fillers" into the remaining VC units boggles the mind. From one point of view, of course, they were Vietnamese from the North helping their brothers in the South. But can you imagine what it would be like to have, say, people from Lancashire in England fill up a guerilla unit in, say, Tennessee? They spoke the same language and they acknowledged the same discipline and loyalty to Ho Chi Minh, but the northerners stuck out like sore thumbs and simply could not pass as belonging to the people of the South.

Now I want to say a little more about each of these trends.

The Four Trends Examined

As regards the growing unpopularity of the war in the United States, public opinion research shows conclusively that Lyndon Johnson misinterpreted not only what happened on the ground during the Tet offensive but also what was happening in the United States, for his own personal popularity declined much more precipitously than support for the war. And even there it depended on how questions were put. The unpopularity of the war was often measured by answers to such questions as, "Do you think the United States made a mistake in sending troops to Vietnam?" Many people, however, including myself, felt on the one hand that it had been a mistake to become involved to such an extent, but at the same time did not want the United States to "bug out" of Vietnam. When the question was asked whether the U.S. should fight on or "end the war even though the Communists might take over sooner or later," advocates of fighting on outnumbered advocates of the latter alternative by two-to-one in 1968. They dropped to a minority in 1971, but they were again the majority in 1972.

Indeed the 1972 election, the smashing defeat of George McGovern as candidate of the Democratic Party, was closely related according to public opinion experts to his advocacy of leaving Vietnam regardless of the consequences. In

1974, finally, when the United States had withdrawn its troops from Vietnam, a majority (oddly enough not a majority of young people) answered "no" to the question whether the U.S. should continue to help the South Vietnamese with military equipment and supplies. Thus it can be said that public support for helping South Vietnam defend itself against aggression lasted for about five

years after Tet, despite appearances to the contrary. It is this discrepancy between appearances and reality that led President Nixon to speak of a "silent majority" that for a long time supported his policies in the war.

Richard M. Nixon

As for the second trend, the growing pressure of inflation, this had to do as already explained with the unwillingness of the government to pay the price. Norman Podhoretz has remarked that both Johnson and Nixon tried to fight the war "on the cheap." This does not mean that we didn't lavish enormous amounts of money on the war. It means that we didn't face the fact that that money had to come from somewhere. Instead of coming out openly and calling for sacrifices on the part of the American people, the money was taken out of their pockets by the most unfair form of taxation, which is inflation. And we paid for the war, also, by weakening our defenses elsewhere. If we have enormous budget deficits now, it is partly because that has to be made up, particularly as the Russians pulled ahead of us during that time.

I was myself appalled for instance by what happened when it was brought out at a meeting of senior officials in Saigon that still more money and equipment were needed for the war, whereupon the Secretary of Defense, Melvin Laird, turned to General Wheeler, the Chairman of the Joint Chiefs of Staff, and said, "Well, we'll just have to take it from NATO." We are still paying in Europe for the policy of robbing Peter to pay Paul; for it was as a result of our concentration on Vietnam, and our failure to pay the price right from the beginning, that our defenses in Europe and elsewhere were so long neglected.

The third trend, the violence of the left wing of the opposition in the United States, was to my mind one of the most fascinating aspects of the war. I have encountered this situation also in other countries during my diplomatic service: When the opposition is filled with a feeling of utter righteousness and certitude, when it displays outrage and high emotion, it obtains a kind of moral ascendancy over those who can defend an ongoing policy only on the grounds that it is neccessary and that it is the least bad of several alternatives.

As I have said, I think the rise of the radical left during the Vietnam War was not really, basically, because of the war.

This view is substantiated by the corresponding rise of a radical left in European countries and Japan at about the same time, unrelated to the issue of Vietnam. Student demonstrations in America were for instance paralleled by student demonstrations in France, which for a while seemed to endanger the Fifth Republic, where the issues were not the same at all.

I would like to tell you a story which has a bearing on this trend. Peter Arnett, correspondent of the Associated Press in Saigon, remarked to a gathering of us in Saigon one evening that on a recent visit to the United States he had encountered Daniel Ellsberg, who had been a passionate believer in what the United States had been doing in Vietnam and who, after his return to the United States and resumption of his academic career, had become one of the signatories of an appeal calling for immediate American withdrawal. How could it happen, he was asked by Arnett, that he had changed so suddenly to the diametrically opposite persuasion? You don't understand, Ellsberg's response is supposed to have been: "Here (and he was referring to his academic environment) you have to be either completely on one side or completely on the other." It seems that among the usually nonconformist intellectual liberal community there was tremendous pressure to conform. Professor Ithiel Pool told me there were even bomb threats against the few proponents of the war on the M.I.T. faculty.

The fourth trend, the amazing progress made by the South Vietnamese government after Tet, is exemplified by two facts: Government control of villages and hamlets rose from somewhere between 40 and 50 percent to about 95 percent. And President Thieu not only expanded his armed forces but also for the first time issued arms directly to the peasants. Over a million rifles were distributed. What government representing a minority and confronted with a popular uprising would dare do such a thing?

The pacification strategy of the Thieu government gave the rural population a stake in their local government, by allowing the elected village councils to decide how to spend government aid, for instance whether to build a new school, an irrigation dike, or a bridge over a canal, so that the result belonged to the community rather than being merely some local manifestation of a bureaucrat in the capital. The result of this program was a steady expansion of security in the countryside and a revival of economic activity there, so that by 1970 even Americans could confidently travel by day or night—even in remote areas of the Mekong delta—and visit villages to see a revival of farms and markets, and schools, and refugees returning from camps to reestablish their homes and family lives. The guerrillas were in most cases not killed, captured or driven away— they were recruited back into village life. So the trend was going very much in favor of the South Vietnamese government in the two years after Tet 1968.

But the electronic media aren't good at reporting trends.

They feed on events that are graphic and if possible dramatic. But even the "slow" media missed, in my opinion, what was a remarkable success story from South Vietnam. And I think there was a good reason for this. People had by that time pretty well made up their minds, especially the people who decide what gets reported and what isn't news. It was about a year after the Tet offensive when one of us at the embassy asked Robert Shaplen, the excellent correspondent of the *The New Yorker* magazine, how it was that he, who had written so many brilliant stories about the situation in Vietnam when things were going badly, hadn't yet filed a story about the remarkable progress that was being made in

South Vietnam in 1969. His reply was that he had written such a story, but *The New Yorker* hadn't published it.

Thieu Government Weaknesses—and Strengths

I don't want to give the impression that there was nothing to criticize in South Vietnam after Tet. Certainly the government of Nguyen Van Thieu had many faults. But it was not oppressive. He took strong measures against the kind of pacifist position that amounted to favoring capitulation to the enemy, but he allowed a large amount of freedom and had an elected parliament (well, elected within certain limits) that certainly gave him frequent major trouble. The fact that newspapers were closed down from time to time could have been taken as an indication that leeway existed for differing opinions, for nobody has ever heard of a newspaper being closed down in a *real* dictatorship because in such a country the government runs the press. There was the usual factionalism and there certainly was corruption, which had long been endemic in that part of the world. So it was easy to report systematically about unpleasantness in South Vietnam, but the basic trend was toward more unity, greater strength, and measurable progress in the fight against the enemy.

Nguyen Van Thieu

South Vietnam had a program allowing VC (and, curiously, also North Vietnamese) to "rally to the government" under an amnesty program called "Chieu Hoi" or "Open Arms." Over the years well over one hundred thousand Viet Cong came in under that program. After 1968 of course there were much fewer VC so there were also fewer defectors from the VC. After Tet there were also beginning to be some desertions among North Vietnamese, and substantial numbers of them became prisoners of war. On the other hand, throughout the war there were many desertions from the South Vietnamese army, but these were not desertions to the enemy; they involved homesick and disgruntled soldiers who went "over the hill" to go home.

It was in this situation, with inconclusive negotiations going on in Paris, that President Nixon decided that the United States could gradually pull out its troops. The program was given the unfortunate name "Vietnamization," which implied that the war somehow had been a non-Vietnamese affair. The withdrawal was gradual, stretching over several years, and it was accompanied by efforts to build up the South Vietnamese armed forces.

The Cambodian Incursion

In 1970 there occurred a totally unexpected change in the government of neighboring Cambodia. When the new Cambodian government of Lon Nol asked the

North Vietnamese to withdraw from their sanctuaries inside Cambodia just across the border from Vietnam, the North Vietnamese turned their full fury on the Cambodians and would have conquered the country in short order if the United States had not helped the Cambodians. But the help was quite limited. One month after the North Vietnamese invasion of Cambodia the South Vietnamese army and some American troops crossed the border into Cambodia in what President Nixon declared to be a limited military action, limited both in time and in distance of penetration, designed both to help the Cambodians and to exploit the fact that the North Vietnamese had left their sanctuaries denuded of troops.

The invasion (or incursion) into Cambodia in 1970 created an explosion of protest in the United States, especially on the campuses. At Kent State University in Ohio the National Guard fired at protesting students and killed four of them. I am showing you this photograph because it is another image that became etched

John Paul Filo

Prize-Winning Photograph

into the consciousness of Americans, showing a girl raising her arms in grief over the corpse of a student. It is, once more, one of those seemingly paradigmatic pictures that turns out to be unrepresentative of what actually happened in the country. Nowhere else in the United States had antiwar protesters resorted to such violence that martial law had had to be declared. At Kent State they had set fire to a building on the campus, and when the fire engines arrived had cut the hoses to prevent the fire's being put out. Nowhere else in the United States had there been a situation in which students then systematically defied martial law. They taunted the young National Guardsmen and pelted them with stones until some of the young and inexperienced Guardsmen broke discipline and fired.

I hope you understand that I am not excusing the shooting. I am just pointing out that in the atmosphere of the time the shooting at Kent State was transformed from an isolated, adventitious happening into something symbolic—the government was made to seem to be using force to suppress dissent and protest. There were even people who thought they saw the ugly face of "fascism" in the beleaguered Nixon administration. In late 1970 antiwar protesters converged on Washington with the intention of paralyzing the capital, for instance by parking automobiles across the roadway on the bridges across the Potomac and throwing the keys into the river.

The 1972 Offensive, and Movement in Negotiations

In 1972, the North Vietnamese launched their biggest offensive of the war up to that time. It was for the most part a conventional offensive with regular divisions attacking from the north, in the central highlands, and along the Cambodian border in the south. American combat troops had by that time withdrawn from Vietnam, and the only support we were able to give the South Vietnamese was from the air, but that support was very effective. President Nixon took the extraordinarily risky decision to mine the ports of North Vietnam, something that the United States had not done before for fear of provoking counteraction from the U.S.S.R. or China. There was no such counteraction. The South Vietnamese first broke and ran in the northernmost part of the country, but then regrouped and in arduous fighting regained all the ground they had lost; and in the south they displayed much heroism in defeating a major armored assault on a town called An Loc, near the Cambodian border. So after prolonged sanguinary fighting, and with American air support, the North Vietnamese offensive was smashed. It was estimated that the North Vietnamese lost 130,000 men killed or disabled. It must have been terribly disillusioning for them to do so badly when American troops were not helping the South Vietnamese any more.

In this situation, and with the public opinion polls showing that the peace-at-any-price candidate, George McGovern, would be badly beaten in the forthcoming election by the incumbent President Nixon, the North Vietnamese for the first time showed flexibility in secret negotiations with Henry Kissinger: Apparently they thought that if Nixon was able to mine the ports and bomb the North with B-52s before the elections, there was no telling what he might do to them after the elections.

The concessions made by the North Vietnamese in these negotiations were quite extraordinary. They accepted a cease-fire-in-place, which they had previously always opposed. They no longer insisted on a political settlement before there could be a cease-fire. They accepted internationally supervised elections, which they had always rejected. And in place of the coalition government which they had advocated (a coalition which would have excluded Thieu) they now were willing to settle for something called a "National Council of National Reconciliation and Concord," a body in which they would sit together with the representatives of the South Vietnamese government and in which the latter would have a veto because decisions would have to be unanimous. All this represented a face-saving retreat for the North Vietnamese, although President Thieu looked especially on the last provision with the utmost suspicion. Finally, whereas earlier the Communists had insisted that the U.S. must not only leave Vietnam but undertake to provide no further support to the South Vietnamese, they now agreed that the government could continue to receive American economic and military assistance within certain limits.

Hanoi was clearly in a hurry to conclude an agreement that would get the Americans completely out of South Vietnam even at the cost of enormous concessions, and they wanted that agreement concluded before the American elections. Everything seemed set for a ceremonial signing in Hanoi on October 31, but then something unexpected happened—when the terms were explained to President Thieu, he rejected them and thereby brought the entire process to a screeching halt. Although he had been kept informed of the negotiations in general terms and had signified his general approval, he now found many things to criticize in the agreement. In vain did Henry Kissinger practice on him his most brilliant advocacy and exegesis, pointing out the many respects in which the Communists had made far-reaching concessions; in vain did he also threaten that the United States might have to go ahead and sign without its South Vietnamese ally. Thieu, who was so widely regarded as a "puppet" of the Americans and who in fact had never been anything of the sort, now dug in his heels. Kissinger had to notify Hanoi that he was sorry, the agreement could not be signed at the contemplated date, and it was necessary to resume the negotiations to "clarify" certain points and make certain "minor" adjustments.

Hitch in the Proceedings

The reaction of the North Vietnamese was to publish the agreement that they had negotiated with the United States, which proved embarrassing in two respects: First, having been scooped by Hanoi, Nixon and Kissinger now had to rush to catch up. Speaking only a few days prior to the 1972 elections Kissinger declared, "I believe peace is at hand," and at a press conference set forth what

Henry A. Kissinger

had been agreed and explained why certain clarifications were still necessary. This was greeted by the opposition in the United States as a blatant attempt to hoodwink the electorate, pretending that an agreement was at hand when in fact divergences still existed. Second, and still more embarrassing, President Thieu compared the Vietnamese-language text broadcast by Radio Hanoi with the English-language text that the Americans had been working with, and he was now able to point to a number of instances where the two did not correspond. There were indeed things that still needed to be negotiated.

I am giving you this in some detail because we are almost at the end of the story of the war in Vietnam. You all know that the agreement, after it was concluded, was immediately and consistently broken by the North Vietnamese. But it was also broken by the South Vietnamese, and, most significant, there was also a clear breach of an important commitment made by the United States. So I hope you will bear with me while I now lead you through some of the intricacies of the remaining negotiations.

At the request of the South Vietnamese, the United States at the reconvened negotiations demanded a number of clarifications and rectifications of the text and also put forward a long list of additional changes desired by the South Vietnamese. Most of those changes were rejected by the other side, but on the whole the resumed negotiations in November 1972 resulted in an improved agreement from the point of view of South Vietnam.

But Thieu was *still* not ready to sign onto the agreement. In order to make him come around the United States stepped up its already gigantic effort to resupply and stock up South Vietnam before the armistice, by airlifting enormous masses of additional war materiel. For instance, we persuaded Taiwan and Iran to give us fighter planes out of their inventory which we could supply to South Vietnam (and which we of course had to replace), as part of an effort to give Thieu and his government increased confidence that they could hold their own against the North Vietnamese after we were gone. But most important in finally obtaining Thieu's agreement was the personal promise from President Nixon, a promise he gave in writing to the South Vietnamese leader, that the United States would provide full military support to South Vietnam in the event of a major violation of the agreement by the North Vietnamese. It was this promise that I was referring to when I said there was also a clear breach of an important commitment by the United States after the abortive peace agreement was signed.

With only a few minor points remaining to be settled, it now turned out that the North Vietnamese had become considerably less interested in an agreement. They said, in effect, that if one side reopens the agreement and seeks improvements from its point of view, the same can be done by the other side; and although from the American point of view only a few minor details remained to be agreed, the North Vietnamese all of a sudden had a whole list of new demands and questions. In addition they asked for a recess in the negotiations, probably to give Hanoi an opportunity to reassess the whole situation.

One can only speculate on what lay behind this drawing back from the agreement on the part of the North Vietnamese. I myself think the major reason was that they had learned from their contacts in the United States that even though President Nixon had been reelected with a large majority in the November elections, the opponents of the war had gained enough additional seats in the House and the Senate so that a good likelihood now existed that when the new Congress convened in January it would proceed to cut off American funds for the war. But there were also other reasons the agreement had become less attractive to the North Vietnamese. The huge American supply effort to South Vietnam was probably an unwelcome surprise for them. The agreement itself had become less attractive to the North to the same extent that it had become more acceptable to the South. And finally there must have been a suspicion on their part that they had been led down the garden path by that wily negotiator Kissinger. They certainly must have found it very difficult to believe that the alleged "lackey" of the Americans, Nguyen Van Thieu, could obstruct the agreement.

The Christmas Bombing

So now everything seemed to unravel again. What could the United States do to bring the North Vietnamese back to the negotiating table and finally button up the agreement? There was nothing more we could offer the North Vietnamese.

We had already hinted broadly to them that there could be large economic benefits for them from a peace agreement. We could not make concessions to them departing from the text as it was negotiated in early December, because in that case we would have again been unable to bring our South Vietnamese ally to sign the agreement. So as an exercise to help the North Vietnamese make up their mind, the President upon recommendation of Kissinger ordered a major bombing campaign by B-52s of military targets in and around the North Vietnamese capital of Hanoi and the port of Haiphong.

This was the so-called Christmas bombing of 1972, reviled around the world as an act of unparalleled barbarism, with accusations that we were "carpet-bombing" the densely populated downtown area of Hanoi and inflicting death and destruction on a scale previously seen only in the fire raids against Dresden and Tokyo and in the nuclear bombing of Hiroshima and Nagasaki. The *New York Times* and *Washington Post*, the major networks, all the prestige media seemed united in terming the bombing campaign criminal, senseless, counterproductive, and exceedingly dangerous because it could provoke counteraction by the Soviet Union or China or both.

But an examination of what really happened shows that the bombing was much more accurate than was believed and of course much more accurate than the North Vietnamese had claimed. The weight of bombs dropped was as great or greater than that dropped on Dresden or Tokyo, but because the bombing was carefully confined to military and military-related targets, the total number of killed in Hanoi was only about 1,300. But the destruction of communications and transport and other military targets was almost complete. And the bombing achieved its political purpose. For the first time it seemed that the United States was willing to pull out all the stops.

The North Vietnamese were deeply impressed by the seriousness with which we viewed their interruption of the negotiations. After ten days of bombardment they asked for the negotiations to be resumed. They then conceded the points that had been outstanding in December and initialed the finished agreement with the U.S. on January 23, 1973. Four days later, after he had been subjected to a combination of American promises and threats, President Thieu with deep misgivings authorized South Vietnam to participate in the formal signing.

From Thieu's point of view the acceptance of the North Vietnamese military presence in South Vietnam was the most deeply troubling element. On the other hand he turned out to be quite wrong about the National Council, which never amounted to anything and had no influence on events. The international supervisory mechanism turned out to be a complete farce. But what might have saved the agreement from being completely overturned— the American threat to return and to give full support to South Vietnam at least in terms of materiel and air support in case North Vietnam launched another offensive—that element became more and more eroded and moot and eventually worthless: President Nixon became ever more preoccupied and weakened by Watergate; the Congress progressively reduced our aid to South Vietnam; and eventually the administration's

hands were tied by legislation that would have in any case made full implementation of President Nixon's promise almost impossible.

It has been said that the agreement of January 1973 was really a hypocritical
exercise designed to provide only a so-called "decent interval" between the
departure of the United States and the takeover by the Communists. I think the
agreement was certainly not a very good one from the point of view of South
Vietnam, but it was the best that could be gotten under the circumstances and
it would have given the South Vietnamese a chance to maintain themselves if
the United States had helped them do so—without troops, of course, but with
the other things that were necessary, including resumed air support if needed. I
don't think it was generally recognized that the deal was really infinitely better
than we had any right to expect, and that it was the result of negotiations in
which Kissinger really distinguished himself.

All the time we had said that the differences over South Vietnam should be
adjudicated by internationally supervised elections, and that was in the agreement. All the time the Communists had insisted that in effect we deliver South
Vietnam to them on a platter—but the agreement left the South Vietnamese
government intact. It is ironical that many of the pundits at home blandly claimed
that we could have gotten the same terms years before, which is complete
nonsense. The terms were the very antithesis of what the North Vietnamese had
been insisting upon for years.

I must show you this comic strip because it exemplifies the attitude of the
critics of the war at that time. It shows the American GI, B.D., walking along
with a North Vietnamese soldier whom he has encountered and befriended and
who miraculously speaks English and has the name Fred, although it is spelled
P-h-r-e-d. The strip has Phred telling B.D.: "You are getting the same terms
you would have gotten four years ago! Why didn't you just pull out then?" To
which B.D. replies with utter outrage: "Are you kidding? And cause a bloodbath?" This was supposed to show up the absurdity of the American position.

I regard Gary Trudeau, the creator of the Doonesbury strip, as an important
American political journalist. Where did he get the information, or rather mis-
information, for this strip? From the newspapers or watching television, of
course. The strip reflects the attitude of cynicism, mingled of course with relief,
that greeted the January 1973 agreement.

Anyway, what about the Christmas bombing? Was it really necessary and was it a success? In terms of the ultimate outcome it turned out that, like so much else in Vietnam, it didn't matter very much. But in terms of its immediate objective it was a classical example of military force used in an impressive but restrained manner to accomplish a precise political objective. Nothing quite like that had happened before. But the electronic media didn't acknowledge the error of their criticisms even when there was no longer any doubt about it. The Pentagon displayed to the press a huge composite photograph of Hanoi taken in January 1973, after the bombing, showing that contrary to what had been claimed there had been no "carpet-bombing" but quite precise hits on designated targets (although of course a few bombs, as usually happens, went astray). The *Washington Post* carried the news about that photograph at the end of a story on another subject on page 24.

When one reads now what some of our most eminent columnists wrote at the time of the bombing, imputing the basest cruelty, stupidity and mendacity to the U.S. government, one becomes rather humble, and perhaps also a bit scared about how the record will look to future historians who use the media archives to reconstruct what happened in the Vietnam War.

Fall of South Vietnam

I think the rest of the story is quickly told. The year 1973 was the year of the Arab-Israeli (Yom Kippur) War and of the "oil shock," when prices went up sixfold. The needs in Vietnam thus increased, but instead the administration's aid requests for Vietnam were cut by the Congress. The President (and thus the authority of the Executive) became more and more mired in the Watergate scandal, which transformed itself from an investigation of political campaign practices into a full-dress investigation of the seamy aspects of the incumbent President's political history. While American aid to Saigon declined, Soviet aid to Hanoi was stepped up. Being safe from effective military opposition in Laos and Cambodia, the North Vietnamese now widened the Ho Chi Minh trail into a regular all-weather road network accompanied by a fuel pipeline from the north all the way to the sanctuaries across the border in the south. They positioned themselves for a major offensive with all the elements of modern ground warfare, including armored divisions, mechanized infantry, the most modern communications, and the tremendous artillery firepower that corresponds to the Soviet order of battle.

And in 1975 they struck. The South Vietnamese army, bereft of the aid it needed from the United States, short on fuel and ammunition, in effect written off by everybody, collapsed first in the highlands, then in the northern provinces, and finally after brief heroic and tragically ineffective resistance, also on the approaches to Saigon. The North Vietnamese army took Saigon, immediately renamed Ho Chi Minh City, on April 30, 1975. As I have already explained, by that time the Viet Cong, the alleged freedom-fighting revolutionary guerrillas of South Vietnam, had been reduced to a minor factor.

To the American public the defeat of our ally was made less shocking by a stream of stories and pictures that cast aspersions on the South Vietnamese army. It was as if some stories had been held back until the debacle was imminent, to make sure that no wave of public opinion favoring help to South Vietnam could develop. So the *New York Times* on its front page pictured a South Vietnamese prisoner-interrogator preparing to hang a VC prisoner who refused to give information— an event highly unlikely to have happened during a broad retreat (if it happened at all). Carefully hoarded stories of past corruption and peculation were ladled out in parallel with the news of South Vietnamese reverses. Malcolm W. Browne, whom we have encountered in connection with his systematic discrediting of Ngo Dinh Diem, had a story, also featured on the front page of the *Times*, about how he encountered a South Vietnamese soldier who was walking toward the front when everyone else was retreating. Asked whether he was rushing to join the fighting he replied, according to Browne, that no, he was just going back to his unit in order to pick up his pay, after which he intended to get out of there like everybody else just as fast as possible.

I don't know if anybody has remarked upon this odd phenomenon before: I believe that during the entire war the American media never featured a story about individual acts of bravery and heroism on the part of our South Vietnamese ally. Yet there were many such acts. When one read about the South Vietnamese army at all, or saw pictures of them, it was usually in connection with defeats, corruption, desertion, cruelty and general ineffectiveness. Yet they took six times the casualties that we took during the war. They had their faults and weaknesses, but they deserve to be remembered as patriots in a lost cause, and perhaps a cause that need not have been lost. In one respect we have, however, done the right thing by the South Vietnamese. In the stampede to get out of South Vietnam before the debacle we did offer asylum in the United States to a substantial number of them. But of course it was only a fraction of those who wanted to get out.

Conclusions

What can we learn from our experience in Vietnam? A great deal, I think. The war taught the world a lot about us, and there are mistakes we made from which we should be able to learn. We should also acknowledge that we did some things right, and try to learn from them also. And much information has become available since the end of the war that also teaches important lessons.

First, it is quite obvious—it had been known for a long time but it now became glaringly apparent—that the United States is not capable of waging a protracted war, and especially not one that is complex and hard to understand and where the good guys don't wear white hats and the bad guys black hats. Any war which is combined with a civil war is difficult for foreigners to understand—the same was true in Greece during World War II and in Yugoslavia. We are just no good in such situations, which require a patient sorting-out of things and working over a long period of time, with mistakes and inevitable injustices in addition to the destruction and pain and suffering that are part of any war.

Second, in spite of all the ambiguities there is really no doubt about which side the people of South Vietnam were on. They were on the side of the South Vietnamese government, and often they "voted with their feet" by streaming to the side that we were defending. There is an important truth here to which I have already referred. Very often one is tempted to conclude that because a particular government isn't popular, therefore its opponents must be popular. Neither Diem nor Thieu nor the other South Vietnamese leaders in between were popular. But people did not take to leaky boats by the hundreds of thousands to escape from their control.

Third, it seems clear to me that we have not solved the problem of electronic media reporting during such a war. This is a big subject, and all I can do is to point out that sooner or later something will have to be done about it. From what I have said earlier I imagine you suspect what it is that I feel the government should have done and what it must be able to do in future situations of this kind.

Fourth, we were often wrong in our appraisal of enemy actions and reactions. It has been said by a critic that if President Johnson had spent as much time studying Vietnamese history and cultural and social patterns as he spent in picking targets for bombing attacks, he would not have escalated the American commitment; but this is very debatable. Secretary of State Dean Rusk said at one time—and I am not quoting his exact words—that we underestimated the tenacity and perseverance of the North Vietnamese; but he added that the North Vietnamese got a lot of unexpected encouragement in their tenacity and perseverance from antiwar activists in the United States, so that it isn't possible to know what they would have done in the absence of such encouragement.

Fifth, it is now established that the Viet Cong and their superstructure, the National Liberation Front (NLF), and *its* superstructure, the "Provisional Revolutionary Government of South Vietnam," were all front organizations of the North Vietnamese with no political life and personality of their own, although they went to great pains to suggest to outsiders that they did have a life and personality of their own. It must have been embarrassing to American opponents of the war who had denied that the war had been started by the North, and who denied that the VC were completely subservient to the North, to have all those things now officially confirmed as true by the Communist government of the united Vietnam. However, like everything else this, too, is subject to some qualification. There were apparently some members of the NLF who actually believed that it was a coalition of equal partners. They are now in jail or dead or, if they are lucky, in exile.

Sixth, the American government was not wrong in picturing the enemy as ruthlessly ideological and bent upon the establishment of a totalitarian regime in the South. It was pitiful to see how some former American opponents of the war appealed to the victors in Hanoi to show a decent respect for human rights, recalling that those antiwar activists had denounced the Thieu government for its lack of freedom and had expected things to improve under the North Vietnamese. Such appeals just showed the signatories to have been very naive, albeit well-meaning. The Communist government of the united Vietnam has turned out to be just as bad as its opponents had feared, with the minor exception that there was no bloodbath. Instead the opponents of the Communist regime—any persons suspected of being opposed—were put into concentration camps.

Seventh, the methods used in the U.S-sponsored pacification program, which eventually involved utmost decentralization and giving more and more responsibility, funds and power to the local communities, worked. In particular the Phoenix program of digging out the VC infrastructure—the roots that they had sunk into the local communities—was extraordinarily effective. The program was maligned on many counts including the charge that it was a program of "assassination." It was nothing of the sort, and its effectiveness has been attested by none other than the Communist General Van Tien Dung in a television interview after the war.

Eighth, and this is most grave, I think the Vietnam War discredited for a while the very idea of collective security. Our disillusionment with Vietnam produced a widespread weariness with foreign commitments and a disgust with what intervention in any war entails. I think typical of this attitude was another Doonesbury cartoon by Gary Trudeau, this one just showing the White House with legends indicating a conversation between President Ford and the NATO ambassadors. The President assures them that the United States will stand by its commitments and is "still prepared to do for France or Britain or Israel what we have done in the past for Indochina." "Do you mean," the ambassadors of free world countries ask, that "we can count on you to interfere in our civil wars and to kill and maim millions of our citizens?" "Exactly!" answers the President. "Whew!" "What a relief!" "That's very reassuring sir," they say. When you think about this little editorial—for the comic strip is a political statement—you can appreciate what the Indochina war did to our moral feelings

DOONESBURY

by Garry Trudeau

of self-worth. Some Americans felt guilty for having helped the South Vietnamese, and regarded the idea of helping our allies elsewhere as somehow morally base and ignoble. Of course it is true that wars kill people. But a country that thinks only in such terms when it comes to helping its friends is in real danger of winding up without any friends.

Ninth, it has been shown that the fear that the Vietnamese Communists would not stop with the conquest of South Vietnam, was not unreasonable. The invasion and occupation of Communist Cambodia by Communist Vietnam has alarmed all the non-Communist states of Southeast Asia. Little Vietnam is not so little anymore. It has a population approximately equal to that of France, and it has the fourth largest army in Asia, one that is experienced and battle-hardened and buoyed up by a succession of victories.

Finally, the Vietnam War has shaken the American consensus about the containment of Communism. I know it is customary and certainly most effective to end such a series of lectures with some short and pithy statement that will encapsulate a central lesson, but I have no central lesson. Instead I will read to you a quotation that to my mind widens the focus again and gives some meaning to what we were about in Vietnam. This is from an article by Irving Kristol, which as far as I know wasn't widely remarked upon and certainly hasn't been reprinted in any of the anthologies of the war; but in my opinion it explains what we conceded to the Communists when we withdrew from Vietnam. Kristol wrote this in 1968 when antiwar sentiment had risen after the Tet offensive:

> . . . Let us put this issue in its strongest terms. Let us concede, for the purposes of argument, that the Vietcong and its allies are fighting a *just* war—that they have some kind of *right* to govern Vietnam, that the people *want* them in power, that the South Vietnamese regime is without *any* claim to legitimacy. I think all of these propositions are false. But what if they were true? How much difference would that make, should that make, to American policy? The answer is: not much.
>
> It is only at first sight, and at first thought, that such an answer is shocking. After all, most of us would agree that the Communist regimes in Poland and Czechoslovakia and East Germany are not more just, or legitimate, or popular than the South Vietnamese regime. Does the United States—or West Germany—thereby have some kind of right to foment civil rebellion and civil war in these countries? To send in arms and soldiers to assist the anti-Communist forces? John Foster Dulles, for a while, talked as if we did. But it was frivolous, irresponsible chatter, and when the chips were down— in East Germany and in Hungary—it was exposed as such.

As an historian and diplomat, and as a teacher, this is the thought I want to leave with you, moving us away from Vietnam and back to the larger picture of East-West relations that I tried to sketch out for you in my second lecture. I don't think Southeast Asia is going to be the place where East-West tensions will threaten to ignite a general war. Whatever validity our experience in Vietnam has must be in terms of what it teaches us about our relationship with the Communist world in other areas, for instance, in Europe and the Middle East.

We—the United States and the other free countries that cooperate with us and depend on us for their security—need some framework of predictable behavior that will keep the danger of general war to a minimum. Our own behavior has been made less predictable by what we have done and failed to do in Vietnam. We tried there to maintain a division of the world with a clear line that could be defended. We failed. I'm not sure we needed to have failed, but that is less important now. The danger in the present situation, which we helped to create by not forcing a stalemate in Vietnam, is that there no longer is a line to hold. The situation has become fluid, and what was inconceivable only a few years ago—for instance that the Soviet Union would occupy a nonaligned country in Asia—has become possible.

I am not wise enough to tell you what can be done to create a new equilibrium of forces now that the old one is gone. All I can do is to point out to you that what happened in Vietnam has had repercussions almost everywhere because it has affected what we think we can and cannot do, just as it has affected what others think they can do with impunity. This is not a good situation, and it cannot last. Either a new equilibrium will be created, which may require greater sacrifices on our part, or there will be more and more Vietnams, some probably closer to home.

About the Author

Born in New York in 1917, Martin F. Herz was educated in Vienna and Oxford and graduated from Columbia University in 1937. During World War II he served for five years in the U.S. Army, where he rose from private to major, was injured in action at Anzio beachhead, and was decorated with the Bronze Star and the Purple Heart. He specialized in psychological warfare and was the author of leaflets dropped by the millions to persuade German soldiers to surrender.

In 1946 he entered the Foreign Service of the United States by examination and served for thirty-three years. His assignments in the Foreign Service included: Third (then Second) Secretary, Political Officer, Vienna; Officer-in-Charge of Austrian Information and Cultural Affairs, Department of State; Second Secretary, Political Officer, Paris; First Secretary, Political Officer, Phnom Penh; First Secretary, Political Officer, Tokyo; United Nations Adviser, Politico-Military Advisor, and Special Assistant for Planning, Bureau of African Affairs, Department of State; Political Counselor, Tehran; Director for Laos-Cambodian Affairs, Department of State; Political Counselor (with rank of Minister), Saigon; Deputy Assistant Secretary of State for International Organization Affairs; Ambassador to the People's Republic of Bulgaria.

From 1978 until his death, Ambassador Herz was Director of Studies of the Institute for the Study of Diplomacy at the Georgetown University School of Foreign Service. He developed the Institute's focus on the operational problems and processes of diplomacy through a ground-breaking series of case studies, symposia and other monographs published by the Institute. Among the twenty-odd publications produced under his tutelage and editorship at the Institute are, to name but a few, *The Modern Ambassador: The Challenge and the Search; Diplomats and Terrorists: What Works, What Doesn't; The Consular Dimension of Diplomacy; Contacts with the Opposition; UN Security Council Resolution 242: A Case Study in Diplomatic Ambiguity; Diplomacy: The Role of the Wife;* and *Resolution of the Dominican Crisis, 1965: A Study in Mediation.* During his years at Georgetown, Ambassador Herz served concurrently as Oscar Iden Research Professor of Diplomacy and taught courses in modern diplomacy and communications, the Cold War, and a senior honors seminar.

A classic example of the diplomat-scholar, Martin Herz was an historian, an educator and a prolific author. He wrote numerous articles that were published in professional journals, magazines and newspapers, such as *Public Opinion Quarterly, Orbis, Military Review, Encounter, Commentary* and others. He played an active role in the American Foreign Service Association and was a frequent contributor to the *Foreign Service Journal.*

His previous books include *The Golden Ladle* (a children's book co-authored with Zack Hanle), 1944; *A Short History of Cambodia,* 1958; *Beginnings of the Cold War,* 1966, 1969; *How the Cold War Is Taught,* 1978; *Decline of the West? George Kennan and His Critics* (editor), 1978; *The Prestige Press and the Christmas Bombing, 1972: Images and Reality in Vietnam,* 1980; and *215 Days in the Life of an American Ambassador,* 1981.

On October 5, 1983, Martin F. Herz died at the age of 66 in Washington, D.C. A memorial fund has been established in his honor at the Institute for the Study of Diplomacy.